A Private Company's Purchase of Own Shares

A Private Company's Purchase of Own Shares

Trevor Johnson FTII AITI ATT

Butterworths
London, Edinburgh and Dublin
1997

United Kingdom	Butterworths, a Division of Reed Elsevier (UK) Ltd, Halsbury House, 35 Chancery Lane, LONDON WC2A 1EL and 4 Hill Street, EDINBURGH EH2 3JZ
Australia	Butterworths, SYDNEY, MELBOURNE, BRISBANE, ADELAIDE, PERTH, CANBERRA and HOBART
Canada	Butterworths Canada Ltd, TORONTO and VANCOUVER
Ireland	Butterworth (Ireland) Ltd, DUBLIN
Malaysia	Malayan Law Journal Sdn Bhd, KUALA LUMPUR
New Zealand	Butterworths of New Zealand Ltd, WELLINGTON and AUCKLAND
Singapore	Reed Elsevier (Singapore) Pte Ltd, SINGAPORE
South Africa	Butterworths Publishers (Pty) Ltd, DURBAN
USA	Michie, CHARLOTTESVILLE, Virginia

A CIP Catalogue record for this book is available from the British Library.

ISBN 0 406 01190 7

Typeset by M Rules
Printed in Great Britain by
Redwood Books, Trowbridge, Wiltshire

Preface

If this work had a sub-title it would probably be 'Everything you never realised you needed to know about a purchase of own shares'. The subject of own share purchases encompasses both company and revenue law. Unfortunately, most tax authors who cover the subject usually do so only as part of some wider topic, and are reluctant to comment on company law in any detail. Phrases appear saying there may be a need to amend the company's Articles without explaining what that amendment should be or how it should be implemented.

When I set out to write this work my objective was to produce a practical guide to all aspects of a private company's purchase of its own shares. I wanted to provide the reader with, not only the basic information on the company and revenue law implications, but also, by means of a collection of precedents, the confidence to provide a complete service to the client. Whilst there may be those advisers who wish to involve another professional in the legal aspects of a transaction, they still need to be able to speak with some authority on those aspects.

I am often frustrated to find reference works which merely paraphrase the legislation; they stick to the well-worn path where others have gone before and never seem to cover the particular point which I need to resolve. At times in this work I have therefore stuck my head above the parapet. This, of course, is a high risk strategy. Whether or not the opinions expressed are sustainable, I hope that they will at least assist readers to reach a reasoned conclusion of their own. Naturally, constructive criticism from readers will be welcomed.

It is with much gratitude that I acknowledge the kind permission of Sweet & Maxwell to quote from *Bramwell: Taxation of Companies and Company Reconstructions* (6th Edition), and that of The Chartered Institute of Taxation to quote from *Taxation Practitioner* of December 1991.

I cannot close without also expressing my thanks to those who, in one form or another, have contributed to the production of this work; my wife Julie ('Mrs TJ') for amending and proof-reading numerous versions over the last few months and tolerating my absence in the office at all hours; my daughter Kate Johnson LLB for the use of her text books on company law and offering advice thereon; my former colleague Peter Shield ATII FCA, now also a tax consultant, for finding the time to read the completed manuscript and point out the odd idiocy; another former colleague, George Lyall, of Dickinson Dees in Newcastle, for free advice on Scots law; Alison Lovejoy of Butterworths for appearing to believe me when I said the book was 'nearly finished'. Finally, but certainly not least, my colleague on the CIOT Council, Jean Jesty BA FTII ATT. Whilst in the midst of establishing her own consultancy practice, she enthusiastically took time out to review my draft manuscripts with meticulous care. She has striven to tactfully unsplit my infinitives and improve the grammar and punctuation. In addition she has challenged some of my idiotic notions on technical matters and found the flaws in my arguments and examples. Any faults found in this work will have been added after Jean's final review and I alone am responsible.

Trevor Johnson

Hoylake

Contents

Table of Statutes

References in the Table to *Statutes* are to Halsbury's Statutes of England (Fourth Edition) showing the volume and page at which the annotated text of the Act may be found.

References in the right-hand column are to paragraph numbers.
References in *italic* type refer to the page numbers of the appendices.

Table of Cases

W

Z

Chapter One

Introduction and Overview

1.1 The ability of a company to purchase its own shares was unknown in this country until the Companies Act 1981 introduced specific legislation.[1] Previously, it had been declared by the House of Lords[2] that it was unlawful for a company to purchase its own shares even though it may have been empowered to do so by its articles. The basic objection to such a transaction arose from the fear that the creditors would not have the protection of the courts against such a reduction of capital. The only permitted way of reducing a company's share capital was by means of a special resolution which had to be confirmed by the court.[3]

1.2 With the protection of creditors in mind, the Companies Act 1981 also introduced strict controls over a company's ability to make use of the relaxations. In considering a possible purchase of own shares from a tax viewpoint, it is easy to overlook the fact that quite often it is the company law requirements which may create greater difficulties than those of tax law. The reason for the changes introduced in 1981 was to encourage more equity investment in smaller businesses by opening up a further exit route for shareholders. The company itself could now be a potential purchaser.

1.3 To complement the changes in company law, which took effect from 15 June 1982, the tax legislation was amended by the Finance Act 1982. Prior to that, even if a purchase of own shares had been lawful, it would have been regarded as a distribution[4] with the result that the shareholder would face an income tax liability at his or her highest rate of tax, less a credit for basic rate tax, and the company would incur a liability to account for advance corporation tax.

1.4 The Finance Act 1982 introduced the concept of an 'exempt distribution' which is only applicable in the case of unquoted companies. It will thus apply to all private companies and to those public companies which are unquoted, the latter category being outside the scope of this work. The exemption took the distribution outside the normal rules and thus removed the income tax charge on the shareholder and the advance corporation tax liability of the

---

1 CA 1985 ss 162 to 181.
2 *Trevor v Whitworth* (1887) 12 App Cas 409.
3 Under what is now CA 1985 s 135.
4 Under what is now TA 1988 s 209(2)(b).

company. As a consequence, the proceeds received by the shareholder became liable to capital gains tax. Previously, because the proceeds attracted an income tax charge, they were exempt from capital gains tax.[1]

1.5 Such is the Inland Revenue's obsession with the possibility that the exemption might be exploited, that exempt distribution status is only available to two kinds of purchases; firstly, those which are intended to be for the benefit of a trade, which do not have as one of their objectives the avoidance of tax and which also satisfy other strict criteria; and secondly, those which are to enable a vendor to meet an inheritance tax liability. Any purchases which do not satisfy these tests remain to be treated as distributions.

1.6 During subsequent chapters, the terms 'distribution treatment' and 'capital treatment' will be used and some explanation of these terms is required:

— 'distribution treatment' refers to the tax treatment of a purchase of own shares which does not qualify as an exempt distribution. As a result, the proceeds are treated as a distribution. Income tax liabilities arise on individual vendors and the purchasing company will have a liability to advance corporation tax. There is, nevertheless, a disposal of the shares for capital gains tax purposes and, usually, a loss will arise since any amounts charged to tax as a distribution are normally excluded from the capital gains tax computation.
— 'capital treatment' refers to the tax treatment of a purchase of own shares which does qualify as an exempt distribution. Such purchases do not give rise to advance corporation tax liabilities on the purchasing company and the entire sales proceeds enter into the capital gains computation of the vendor.

1.7 When the legislation permitting a company to purchase its own shares was first introduced in 1982, there was a clear advantage in the exempt distribution or capital treatment; capital gains tax was a flat rate of 30% and the highest rate of income tax was 75%. Since the unification of income and capital gains tax rates in 1989, there are now often cases where exempt distribution status is a positive disadvantage and deliberate steps may have to be taken in order not to satisfy the criteria!

1.8 This bizarre situation is evidenced by the fact that not only is it possible to apply for advance clearance that capital treatment will apply, it is also possible to apply for negative clearance, ie that capital treatment is not available. Nevertheless, despite all the restrictions imposed by the Revenue, a purchase of own shares, whatever its tax treatment, can, in the right circumstances, be a tax-efficient method of achieving a number of objectives. This work is intended to be a practical guide to the possibilities and pitfalls of a purchase of own shares which are likely to be faced by practitioners in the majority of cases involving private companies. No consideration will therefore be given to those aspects of company law which are peculiar to public companies.

---

1 Under what is now TCGA 1992 s 37.

1.9 Perhaps it should be made clear at this point that, whilst company law distinguishes between public and private companies, the tax regime distinguishes between quoted and unquoted companies.[1] Whilst it is theoretically possible to have a public company which is unquoted, it is not possible for a private company to be quoted as such a company is prohibited from offering its shares to the public. The assumption throughout this work is that the situations being considered involve companies which are private and unquoted.

1.10 Company law permits companies to purchase their own shares and to issue (and by implication, redeem) redeemable shares and to fund that purchase or redemption, if it so chooses, out of the proceeds of an issue of further shares. Lawyers may, and indeed do, debate at length the distinction between a purchase and a redemption. For all practical purposes, however, no distinction will be made between a purchase and a redemption unless the context so requires. As will be seen in the context of corporate vendors, the Revenue's opinion is that there is a difference between a purchase and a redemption.

1.11 Additionally, the financing of a purchase or redemption by means of a new issue of shares is covered because, in the context of a private company, it may be the continuing shareholders who have to provide the finance, and commercially, it may be desirable, or indeed necessary, for those funds to be introduced as share capital.

---

1 'Quoted' in this context means quoted in the Official List of The Stock Exchange. A company quoted on the Alternative Investment Market is not regarded by the Inland Revenue as 'quoted'.

Chapter Two

Company Law Requirements

2.1 The requirements of the Companies Act are of paramount importance. This may be difficult for tax advisers to appreciate, but failure to observe the requirements of the Taxes Act will merely lead to an unexpected tax liability. Failure to observe the Companies Act requirements could, at worst, mean 'Go directly to Jail; Do not pass Go'.

ARTICLES OF ASSOCIATION

2.2 Under company law a company is only empowered to purchase or redeem its own shares if it is also authorised to do so by its Articles.[1] Although the ability to purchase own shares was available from 1982, no amendments were made to CA 1948, Sch 1 Table A until 1 July 1985.[2] Between 1982 and 1985 companies being formed would normally have a specific power inserted into their Articles. Companies formed since 1985 will have the following power in their Articles as a matter of course if they have adopted Table A;

> Subject to the provisions of the Act, the company may purchase its own shares (including any redeemable shares) and, if it is a private company, make a payment in respect of the redemption or purchase of its own shares otherwise than out of distributable profits of the company or the proceeds of a fresh issue of shares.[3]

However any company incorporated before July 1985 which has not subsequently adopted new Articles will need to include such a power before any purchase of own shares can be approved.

2.3 If it is necessary to amend the Articles, the members will have to pass a special resolution[4] in a general meeting following which a copy of the new Articles and the special resolution must be filed with the Registrar of Companies within 15 days.[5] A private company can also adopt new Articles

1 CA 1985 s 162(1).
2 The Companies (Tables A to F) Regulations 1985 SI 1985/805.
3 The Companies (Tables A to F) Regulations 1985 SI 1985/805, Table A reg 35.
4 CA 1985 s 9.
5 CA 1985 ss 18(2) and 380(1).

by means of a written resolution which avoids the need for a meeting of the shareholders.

2.4 As a special resolution is also required to approve and authorise a purchase of own shares, the resolution to amend the Articles can be passed at the same time and in the same manner as (but preferably before!) the resolution to approve the purchase. The mechanics of passing a special resolution are dealt with later in this chapter beginning at paragraph **2.15**. The only point to make here is that all shareholders are able to vote on the resolution to amend the Articles whereas the vendor shareholder should not vote on the resolution to authorise the purchase.

SPECIFIC CONDITIONS

2.5 Despite the existence of the power within the Articles, certain overriding conditions limit a company's ability to purchase or redeem its own shares:

1 it cannot purchase any shares which are only partly-paid.[1] This is unlikely to be a problem in the vast majority of private companies;
2 payment for the shares must be made in cash and in full on completion of the purchase.[2] The Act says that the terms of the purchase or redemption must provide for 'payment' on completion/redemption. The suggestion is that 'payment' denotes a cash payment which would also fit in with the general intention of the Companies Act. This is also the view of the Revenue who have indicated that capital treatment will only be given in the case of a purchase or redemption which is valid under company law and therefore, inter alia, one where the purchase is for a cash consideration;[3]
3 a purchase may not be effected if, as a consequence, there would no longer be a member holding irredeemable shares.[4] In other words, it is not possible for the company to exist without a shareholder.

FINANCING THE PURCHASE

2.6 The company must account for the purchase in one of three ways:

1 out of distributable profits;
2 out of the proceeds of a fresh issue of shares made specifically for the purpose;[5] or
3 out of capital.[6]

---

1 CA 1985 s 159(3).
2 CA 1985 s 159(3).
3 *Inland Revenue Tax Bulletin*, Issue 21, February 1996 p280; see also Inland Revenue Corporation Tax Manual CT 1750.
4 CA 1985 s 162(3).
5 CA 1985 s 160(1)(a).
6 CA 1985 s 171(1).

2.7 The procedures to follow in the case of a purchase out of distributable profits or out of the proceeds of a fresh issue of shares are identical and will be considered as one. Discussion of the procedures necessary for the issue of new shares is contained in Chapter Eleven.

2.8 It is not absolutely essential that there should be sufficient distributable profits to match the consideration for the purchase but if there are, life is much simpler. There must however be sufficient cash resources which, of course, is not the same thing as distributable profits. Because of the age old need to protect the creditors against reductions in the company's capital, there are more conditions to satisfy in a purchase where there are insufficient distributable profits; in such a case a longer timescale is required to achieve the final result. It is therefore preferable to look at the two scenarios separately.

PURCHASE OUT OF DISTRIBUTABLE PROFITS OR PROCEEDS OF A SHARE ISSUE

2.9 The first question must be 'What are the distributable profits of the company?' These are defined as those profits out of which a company could lawfully make a distribution[1] and are the accumulated realised profits less accumulated realised losses.[2] The emphasis here is on the words 'accumulated' and 'realised'. 'Accumulated' means that any prior years' losses need to be made good before distributions can be made out of current year profits, whilst 'realised' means that only profits realised by the company's accounting reference date can be included in the profit and loss account. The question as to whether profits have been realised or not is to be determined under generally accepted accounting principles. Thus, the revenue reserves shown in the company's last statutory accounts should form the basis of any decision as to whether there are sufficient profits available. But is that sufficient?

2.10 Assuming that the last accounts showed retained profits of £750,000 and the purchase is going to cost £200,000, then, even if the previous balance sheet is nearly a year old, the directors are probably safe in proceeding with the purchase, providing they are satisfied that there have been no horrendous losses incurred since that balance sheet date.

2.11 A different situation would arise where retained profits are only £150,000. In such circumstances the purchase can only proceed as one partly out of capital. There is however nothing to prevent the company preparing a set of interim audited accounts to establish a more accurate, and perhaps adequate, figure of retained profits. If, nevertheless, the retained profits thus disclosed are inadequate then, as we shall see later, those accounts will still be required for a purchase partly out of capital.

---

1 CA 1985 s 181(a).
2 CA 1985 s 263(3).

2.12 Should it happen that the company does make an illegal distribution, then not only will the purported purchase be invalid, but the directors could be called upon to make good the distribution, or that part of it which is illegal, to the company. There is clearly a considerable responsibility upon the directors to ensure that a legal distribution is being made. They in turn will rely upon their auditors to provide some comfort as to the level of distributable profits.

2.13 Where a company has been able to dispense with the need to appoint auditors the directors' responsibilities are even greater. Where there is any doubt as to whether there are sufficient distributable profits, there seem to be only two choices available:

1 to appoint auditors to prepare accounts which will give more comfort to the directors (and if it turns out to be a purchase partly or wholly out of capital, auditors will be required anyway); or
2 for the remaining shareholders to contribute more capital by subscribing for additional shares.

This latter route might be necessary to provide the finance for the purchase. Whilst these funds could be introduced by the continuing shareholders as loan capital, it may be more acceptable from the point of view of the company's bank for this to be share capital.

2.14 Having established that the company's Articles contain the power to purchase its own shares and that the company has sufficient distributable profits with which to make the purchase, or that sufficient funds will be generated from a fresh issue of shares, attention can then be given to the mechanics of the purchase itself.

Special resolution

2.15 The Companies Act requires the proposed contract between the shareholder and the company to be approved in advance by the members by means of a special resolution.[1] This requires 75% of the votes eligible to be cast on the question to be in favour and normally involves the calling of an Extraordinary General Meeting (EGM) by giving 21 days written notice.[2] This notice can be dispensed with if the majority of the members, holding more than 95% of the votes, agree.[3] A private company can in fact use a percentage of not less than 90%, if the members resolve to do so by means of an elective resolution. However as such a resolution needs to be passed at a meeting for which 21 days notice is also required,[4] there seems little point in passing an elective resolution simply to deal with a single transaction.

1 CA 1985 s 164(2).
2 CA 1985 s 378(2); the resolution could be passed at the Annual General Meeting, if one is held, provided that the timing was convenient.
3 CA 1985 s 369.
4 CA 1985 s 379A(2).

2.16 A copy of the proposed contract or a memorandum of its terms must be available for inspection by any member at the registered office for at least 15 days prior to the meeting and at the meeting itself. If the contract does not separately identify the shareholders to which the contract relates, there must be a written memorandum attached showing this information.[1]

2.17 The resolution will not be effective if the vendor shareholder has voted on the resolution and it could not have been carried without the votes attaching to the shares which are the subject of the proposed contract.[2] This prohibition is in respect of the votes attaching to the specific shares which are to be purchased, rather than a general prohibition of the shareholder concerned. If vendors need to exercise vote in respect of shares which are not the subject of the resolution, they would have to demand a poll as it is felt that they would be unable to vote at all on a show of hands.

2.18 Since 15 July 1992, it has been possible for private companies to exist with only one member.[3] A member of such a company could therefore carry a special resolution to sell 99% to the company, provided that he or she only exercised the votes attaching to the 1% he intended to retain. Of course, technically he or she would have to demand a poll for the same reasons as mentioned above. The single member is, in any event, prohibited from passing a resolution to sell a 100% holding as there must always be some irredeemable shares left in issue.

2.19 The special resolution must be filed with the Registrar of Companies within 15 days of it being passed.[4]

Written resolution

2.20 The preferred approach may be to save time and avoid the need for a meeting by passing a written resolution.[5] Under this procedure, the company should send a copy of the proposed contract (together with any necessary attached memorandum)[6] to each member eligible to vote, together with a copy of the written resolution for their signature and return. Such a resolution requires the unanimous consent of the members.[7] For these purposes, the vendor shareholder is not regarded as a member who is eligible to vote.[8] The prohibition in this case applies to the member, not the shares, and therefore a written resolution cannot be used in the case of a single member company.

2.21 If the company has not dispensed with the need to appoint auditors, or is not eligible to do so,[9] the auditors have to be informed of the terms of the proposed written resolution before the resolution is sent to the members for

1 CA 1985 s 164(6).
2 CA 1985 s 164(5).
3 The Companies (Single Member Private Limited Companies) Regulations 1992 SI 1992/1699.
4 CA 1985 s 380(4)(a).
5 CA 1985 s 381A.
6 See para 2.16.
7 CA 1985 s 381A(1).
8 CA 1985 Sch 15A para 5(2).
9 The Companies Act 1985 (Audit Exemption) Regulations 1994 SI 1994/1935.

signature. There is however no need for the auditors to take any action for the resolution to have effect. Prior to 19 June 1996 they had a right to give notice to the company that a general meeting of the company should be held to consider the resolution and to be present at that meeting.

2.22 Strangely, failure to advise the auditors of the proposed resolution does not invalidate it, but any director or secretary of the company is guilty of an offence if he or she knows that a written resolution is to be proposed, knows the terms of that resolution and fails to notify the auditors.[1]

2.23 Once passed, the written resolution must be filed with the Registrar of Companies within 15 days.[2]

The form of the contract

2.24 Whilst a purchase of own shares may only proceed if there is a 'contract' which has received advance approval by the members,[3] there is no requirement that the contract should take any specific form. Indeed the situation is envisaged where the proposed contract is not in writing and in such a case, a memorandum of the terms of the proposed contract should be available for inspection prior to and at the meeting at which the Special Resolution is passed.[4] Although prudence might dictate that a written contract is desirable if only 'for the avoidance of doubt', there seems to be nothing within contract or company law to prevent the directors of the company from entering into a verbal (or 'parol') contract for the purchase of the shares.

2.25 The Companies Act 1985, as amended, specifically provides that in England and Wales, a contract involving a company may be effected either *in writing* under seal by the company itself or, on behalf of the company, by any person acting under its authority.[5] Any contracts made by or on behalf of a company are subject to the same legal formalities as contracts made by individuals. It is therefore possible for a verbal contract to be entered into on behalf of (but clearly not by) a company by a duly authorised director or officer.

2.26 The position in Scotland is identical, although not spelt out as such in the Companies Act. Prior to 31 July 1990, the Act provided that:

> 'Contracts made on behalf of a company may be made as follows –
>
> . . .
>
> (c) a contract which if made between private persons would by law be valid although made by parol only, and not reduced into writing, may be made by parol on behalf of the company by any person acting under its authority, expressed or implied'[6]

---

1 CA 1985 s 381B as amended by The Deregulation (Resolutions of Private Companies) Order 1996 SI 1996/1471 art 3.
2 CA 1985 s 380(1).
3 CA 1985 s 164(1).
4 CA 1985 s 164(6).
5 CA 1985 s 36.
6 CA 1985 s 36(1)(c) – as originally enacted.

This provision was not in any way restricted to any particular legal system. As a parol contract is valid under Scots law, one could therefore be concluded by the directors on behalf of the company. This provision was repealed[1] and replaced with the current version which simply covers the position in England and Wales, whilst a new section was added[2] dealing with the execution of documents in Scotland. It would seem that during this process the position of parol contracts in Scotland was overlooked. Despite the absence of any specific provision to acknowledge that a company's directors can conclude a parol contract, it is felt that this must follow from the fact that such contracts are valid under Scots law and the directors will have the specific authority of a shareholder's resolution.

2.27 Until the special resolution is passed, the director or officer does not have any authority to enter into such a contract. Any previous verbal agreement between the vendor shareholder and the officer would not constitute a contract. It would seem that they need to meet again, after the special resolution had been passed, in order to enter into the verbal contract upon the terms contained in the memorandum approved by the shareholder's meeting. In practice it must be rare if they ever do meet and formally make an offer and an acceptance. The mere fact that the shareholder hands over the share certificate and is paid the purchase price should be sufficient evidence that a verbal contract took place, even though there may not have been one particular conversation which one could point to as being that in which the contract was concluded. The contract would be a verbal one, even if the parties did not realise it. Therefore in many cases, such as where it is the majority shareholder who is retiring (and everyone else is relieved to see him go), a written contract is not absolutely necessary and a memorandum of terms is all that is required. Conversely if there is any friction between the departing shareholder and those remaining then a written contract must be advisable.

2.28 Sometimes what is required is the ability for shares to be purchased on the occurrence of some contingency or for purchases to be staggered over a period. In such cases it is permissible for 'contingent purchase' contracts to be entered into which, of themselves, do not amount to a contract for sale but under which the company may become entitled, or obliged, to purchase the shares.[3] The most obvious example would be put and call options. Such arrangements would still need to be approved in advance by means of a special resolution.[4]

PURCHASE WHOLLY OR PARTLY OUT OF CAPITAL

2.29 Because of the need for creditor protection, a purchase of own shares is hedged around with more restrictions where there are insufficient

1 By Companies Act 1989 s 130.
2 CA 1985 s 36B.
3 CA 1985 s 165(1).
4 CA 1985 s 165(2).

distributable profits or where it is not proposed to finance the purchase out of a new issue of shares. Compliance with these conditions also means that a longer timescale is needed to carry out such a purchase.

The relevant accounts

2.30 Accounts must be available to enable the directors to make 'a reasonable judgement' of the amounts of profits, losses, assets and liabilities; provisions for depreciation, diminution of value of assets, and retentions to meet liabilities; share capital and reserves, including undistributable reserves.[1] Those accounts must be to a date not earlier than three months before the date of the directors' statutory declaration (see below).[2] This judgement is necessary in order to determine the 'permissible capital payment' which is the amount of the share purchase consideration in excess of the company's distributable profits or the proceeds of any fresh issue of shares.[3]

2.31 Clearly, if the proposed purchase is planned for a date later than three months from the last balance sheet date, then accounts will have to be specifically prepared for this purpose. As will be seen later, the auditors will be required to issue a certificate and state that the permissible capital payment has been properly determined. Therefore such accounts should be prepared to the same standards as audited accounts in order that the auditors may satisfy themselves that they have 'enquired into the company's affairs'.

The directors' statutory declaration

2.32 Within three months of the end of the period covered by the relevant accounts, the directors must make a statutory declaration before a Commissioner for Oaths on Form 173 which specifies:

1 the amount of the permissible capital payment;
2 that they have made 'full enquiry into the affairs and prospects of the company'; and
3 that they have formed the opinion that,
   '(a) as regards its initial situation immediately following the date on which the payment out of capital is proposed to be made, that there will be no grounds on which the company could then be found unable to pay its debts; and
   (b) as regards its prospects for the year immediately following that date, that, having regard to their intentions with respect to the management of the company's business during that year and to the amount and character of the financial resources which will in their view be available to the company during that year, the company will still be able to carry on business as a going concern and will accordingly be able to pay its debts as they fall due throughout that year.'[4]

---

1 CA 1985 s 172(3).
2 CA 1985 s 172(6).
3 CA 1985 s 172(4).
4 CA 1985 s 173(3).

2.33 In other words, the directors are declaring that not only will the company still be able to pay its debts immediately after the purchase of the shares, but also for the following 12 months. This is, of course, not something to be entered into lightly, especially as a director making such a declaration without reasonable grounds is liable to imprisonment of up to two years or a fine or both.[1]

The auditor's report

2.34 The directors' statutory declaration must have annexed to it a report from the company's auditors addressed to the directors stating:

1 that they have enquired into the company's state of affairs;
2 that the amount specified as the permissible capital payment for the shares in question is, in their view, properly determined in accordance with sections 171 and 172; and
3 that they are not aware of anything to indicate that the opinion expressed by the directors in the declaration as to any of the matters mentioned therein is unreasonable in all the circumstances.[2]

In contrast to the position on the directors' statutory declaration, there are no specific penalties for auditors who issue a report without reasonable grounds.

2.35 As this legislation was originally introduced in 1981, it might be asked how this fits in, if at all, with the recent changes allowing certain private companies to dispense with auditors.[3] The answer is that no amendment has been made to the purchase of own shares legislation and, consequently, a company which has dispensed with the need to appoint an auditor cannot repurchase its shares out of capital. This fits in with the whole scheme of a purchase out of capital which is conditional upon ensuring protection of the company's creditors. Such a company will therefore need to appoint, or re-appoint, auditors in order to comply with this requirement.

The special or written resolution

2.36 The purchase out of capital must be approved by a special resolution passed either on the same day as the directors' statutory declaration or within the week following.[4] As we are concerned with private companies, the resolution may be passed by way of a written resolution[5] in which case the directors' statutory declaration and auditors' report should be sent to the members with the resolution.

---

1 CA 1985 s 173(6).
2 CA 1985 s 173(5).
3 The Companies Act 1985 (Audit Exemption) Regulations 1994 SI 1994/1935.
4 CA 1985 s 174(1).
5 As previously described at paragraph 2.20.

The *Gazette*

2.37 Within a week of the passing of the resolution, a notice must be published in the *London Gazette* or *Edinburgh Gazette*, as appropriate:

1 stating that the company has approved a payment out of capital for the purpose of acquiring its own shares;
2 specifying the amount of the permissible capital payment and the date of the special resolution;
3 stating that the directors' statutory declaration and auditor's report are available for inspection at the company's registered office; and
4 stating that any creditor may, at any time within the five weeks following the date of the special resolution, apply to the court under s 176 for an order prohibiting the payment.[1]

2.38 The same notice must also be published in an 'appropriate national newspaper', again within a week of passing the resolution.[2] This is defined as circulating 'throughout' England and Wales, or Scotland in the case of a Scottish registered company.

2.39 The objective behind this publicity and the five week breathing space is clearly the protection of creditors. It allows any creditor to apply to the court for an order preventing the purchase or redemption. It also permits a dissenting member of the company to apply to the court for an order, provided he or she did not consent to or vote in favour of the resolution.[3]

2.40 If the worst happens and a creditor or member does apply for an order prohibiting the payment, the company has to give notice of the fact to the Registrar of Companies and deliver to the Registrar a copy of any order made by the court within 15 days of that order being made.[4] The court may cancel or confirm the resolution or sanction an arrangement whereby the dissident creditor may be protected or the member's interests may be purchased.[5]

Returns to Companies House

2.41 Not later than the date of the first of the notices in the *Gazette* and the national newspaper, the directors' statutory declaration and auditor's report must be delivered to the Registrar of Companies.[6]

2.42 From that date onwards and until the end of five weeks from the date of the resolution, the directors' statutory declaration and auditor's report have to be available at the company's registered office for inspection, free of charge, by any member or creditor.[7]

---

1 CA 1985 s 175(1).
2 CA 1985 s 175(2).
3 CA 1985 s 176(1)(a).
4 CA 1985 s 176(3).
5 CA 1985 s 177.
6 CA 1985 s 175(5).
7 CA 1985 s 175(6).

COMPLETION

2.43 The payment out of capital must take place no earlier than five weeks and no later than seven weeks after the date of the special resolution and must be made in full on completion. The vendor should deliver up to the company his or her share certificate.[1]

2.44 There is some difference of opinion as to whether or not a share transfer form is required in the case of a purchase (it being accepted that none is required in the case of a redemption). Those who support the need for such a form argue that as the transaction is described as a 'purchase', it must follow that the company acquires the shares and therefore they must be transferred by a 'proper instrument of transfer.'[2] As will be seen later, the Revenue do not regard any document used to effect completion as being liable to ad valorem stamp duty. The pragmatic view is therefore that no share transfer form is required. A return on Form 169 is required to be delivered to the Registrar of Companies within 28 days of completion and this Form has to be stamped with duty at ½% .[3]

TIMESCALE

2.45 As will be seen, because of the publicity required, a purchase out of capital is quite time consuming and at the very earliest cannot be completed in less than five weeks from the balance sheet date of the relevant accounts. This ignores the time taken to obtain a Revenue clearance, usually 30 days, and the time to prepare a set of audited accounts where the previous accounts were to a date more than three months prior to the directors' statutory declaration. It also assumes that the special resolution would be passed, and the statutory declaration, auditors report and notices and returns would be made on the same day as the relevant accounts became available.

CONSEQUENCES

2.46 Upon completion the shares purchased or redeemed are treated as cancelled[4] and thus the company's issued share capital is reduced by the nominal value of the cancelled shares.

2.47 Because of the need to maintain the company's capital and thereby protect, as far as it is able, the creditors, company law contains specific rules regarding the creation of a capital redemption reserve. This is to be treated as if it were share capital and subject to the normal rules about reduction of capital, but it may also be applied in paying up unissued shares as bonus shares.[5]

---

1 CA 1985 s 174(1).
2 CA 1985 s 183(1).
3 FA 1986 s 66.
4 CA 1985 s 160(4) as applied by s 162(2).
5 CA 1985 s 170(4).

2.48 Where the purchase is *wholly* out of distributable profits an amount equal to the nominal value of the shares cancelled is to be transferred to a capital redemption reserve.[1]

Example

A company purchases 50,000 £1 shares for £250,000, the company's capital would be:

Before		*After*	
Share capital	100,000	Share capital	50,000
Distributable profits	470,000	Distributable profits	220,000
		Capital redemption reserve	50,000
	570,000		320,000

2.49 Where the purchase is either wholly or partly out of capital and the part paid out of capital is less than the nominal value of the shares, the amount of the shortfall must be transferred to the capital redemption reserve.[2]

Example

Assume the facts as in the previous example but distributable profits are only £230,000:

Before		*After*	
Share capital	100,000	Share capital	50,000
Distributable profits	230,000	Distributable profits	Nil
		Capital redemption reserve	30,000
	330,000		80,000

2.50 However, where the purchase out of capital is greater than the nominal value of the shares, the excess may be deducted from any capital reserve, share premium account, issued fully paid-up shared capital or revaluation reserve.[3]

Example

Assume the facts as before except that distributable profits are only £170,000:

Before		*After*	
Share capital	100,000	Share capital	20,000
Distributable profits	170,000	Distributable profits	Nil
	270,000		20,000

1 CA 1985 s 170(1).
2 CA 1985 s 171(4).
3 CA 1985 s 171(5).

2.51 Where the purchase is funded wholly or partly out of the proceeds of a fresh issue of shares and the amount of those proceeds is less than the nominal value of the shares purchased, that shortfall is to be transferred to capital redemption reserve.[1]

Example

Assume the facts as previously described in paragraph 2.50 but that distributable profits are £270,000 and the purchase is partly financed by the issue of £10,000 £1 shares at par.

Before		*After*	
Share capital	100,000	Share capital	60,000
Distributable profits	270,000	Distributable profits	30,000
		Capital redemption reserve	40,000
	370,000		130,000

However this does not apply if the proceeds of the fresh issue are used in addition to a payment out of capital.[2] In such a case the proceeds of the share issue are to be treated for these purposes as being a payment out of capital.[3]

DISCLOSURE IN ACCOUNTS

2.52 Where a company acquires its own shares by purchase, the directors' report has to state the number and nominal value of the shares purchased, the amount of the purchase price and the reasons for the purchase,[4] and also the number and nominal value of those purchased shares which have been cancelled in the year.[5] As all shares purchased have to be cancelled, the numbers and nominal values in both cases should be the same.

WHEN IT ALL GOES HORRIBLY WRONG . . .

2.53 There is a general prohibition on companies acquiring their own shares except, inter alia, when purchased or redeemed in accordance with the provisions previously described.[6] Should any of the requirements fail to be observed, not only will the purchase be invalid, but the company will be liable to a fine and every officer of the company who is in default will be liable to imprisonment or a fine or both. The specific penalties prescribed are as follows:[7]

1 CA 1985 s 170(2).
2 CA 1985 s 170(3).
3 CA 1985 s 171(6).
4 CA 1985 Sch 7 para 8(a).
5 CA 1985 Sch 7 para 8(d).
6 CA 1985 s 143(1).
7 CA 1985 Sch 24.

1 company acquiring its own shares in breach of the conditions of CA 1985, ss 159–181: on indictment, an unlimited fine for the company, two years imprisonment or an unlimited fine or both for the officers; on summary conviction, a fine of £5,000 for the company and six months' imprisonment or a fine of £5,000 or both for the officers;
2 failure to deliver Form 169 to the Registrar of Companies: a fine of £5,000 and a daily default fine of £500 for continued contravention;
3 failure to display a copy of the contract at the company's registered office or refusal to allow an inspection of the contract by a member: a fine of £1,000 and a daily default fine of £100;
4 statutory declaration made by directors without having reasonable grounds for the opinion expressed: on indictment, two years' imprisonment or a fine or both; on summary conviction, six months' imprisonment or a fine of £5,000 or both;
5 refusal to allow any member or creditor to inspect the directors' statutory declaration (certifying the permitted capital payment) and auditor's report: a fine of £400 and a daily default fine of £40;
6 failure to notify the Registrar of Companies of a member's application to the court to cancel the resolution to purchase shares by means of a payment out of capital, or failure to notify the Registrar of any court order resulting from such an application: a fine of £1,000 and a daily default fine of £100; and
7 non-compliance with requirements as regards the contents of the directors' report: every director liable to an unlimited fine on indictment or £5,000 on summary conviction.

Chapter Three

TAXATION: DISTRIBUTION TREATMENT

3.1 Prior to FA 1982, even if a purchase of own shares could legally have taken place, this would have been treated as a distribution[1] involving an advance corporation tax liability for the company and an income tax liability for the shareholder under Schedule F.[2] This situation arises because the definition of a distribution is 'any distribution of assets by a company in respect of shares in excess of a repayment of share capital or new consideration'. In simple terms, the excess of the sales proceeds over the original capital subscribed is a distribution.

3.2 'New consideration' is defined as consideration which is not provided directly or indirectly out of the assets of the company.[3] In particular, it excludes amounts retained by the company by way of capitalising a distribution; in other words, distributable profits which are capitalised in paying up a bonus issue are excluded from being 'new consideration'. It is unlikely to be a feature of a purchase of own shares.

REPAYMENT OF SHARE CAPITAL

3.3 There is no definition within the Taxes Acts of what constitutes a repayment of share capital. In the context of company law it involves the reduction of a company's issued share capital and the repayment of that amount to the shareholders. In essence it is merely returning to the shareholders the amount originally subscribed for the shares, although, of course, the identity of those shareholders may well have changed since the shares were issued. Where shares have previously been issued at a premium, the amount of the premium is regarded as forming part of the issue price of that share capital for the purposes of deciding if there has been a repayment of share capital.[4] Logic says that if a company has received £1 for a £1 ordinary share and purchases that share back again for £1, there has been no distribution out of the assets of the company and it has simply returned the capital it had previously received. Therefore in a straightforward case only the excess

1 TA 1988 s 209(2)(b).
2 TA 1988 s 20.
3 TA 1988 s 254(1).
4 TA 1988 s 211(5).

of the purchase price over the nominal value of the shares purchased will rank as a dividend.

3.4 The vendor's actual 'profit' on the transaction will depend upon whether he or she originally subscribed for the shares or purchased them from a previous holder at a price in excess of nominal value. However, because the distribution legislation looks solely at the position from the company's point of view, the shareholders may be liable to income tax on amounts which have no basis in logic or equity.

3.5 The basic rule in a purchase of own shares is that the distribution is the amount of the proceeds in excess of any repayment of share capital. The position gets complicated where shares have been issued as fully paid up by capitalising profits which could otherwise have been distributed as dividends. It would be illogical to allow the full nominal value of the shares being purchased to be treated as repayment of share capital. As a result, complex rules apply in situations where bonus shares have been issued before, or are issued following, a purchase or redemption of own shares.

Purchase or redemption following earlier bonus issue

3.6 The basic rule on distributions is modified where a company has at any time after 6 April 1965 issued bonus shares which were not at the time of issue treated as a distribution.[1] That part of the proceeds of the purchase of own shares which is equal to their nominal value will not be regarded as a repayment of share capital, except to the extent that those proceeds exceed paid up share capital on the earlier bonus issue.[2] Putting that in simpler terms, the special rule 'disallows' the nominal value of the shares purchased from being regarded as repayments of share capital. The rule will cease to apply once the cumulative total of disallowed nominal value reaches the amount of the retained profits used to pay up the previous bonus issue.

3.7 Apart from the fact that bonus issues prior to 6 April 1965 are ignored[3] (and thereby in effect allowing proceeds equal to their nominal value to be repayments of share capital), there is no time limit for the operation of this provision.[4] When contemplating any purchase of own shares where distribution treatment may be applied, it is necessary to review the company's share history back to incorporation, or 6 April 1965 if later.[5]

3.8 The Revenue's view of the operation of the rules in these circumstances is that no part of the sales proceeds can be regarded as a repayment of share capital whilst the cumulative total of what would otherwise have been a repayment of share capital is less than the nominal value of the bonus shares.

---

1 Under TA 1988 s 210.
2 TA 1988 s 211(1).
3 TA 1988 s 211(1)(a).
4 At least not for unquoted companies – see TA 1988 s 211(2).
5 Inland Revenue Company Taxation Manual CT 1540.

Their view is also that the number of shares sold cannot be identified with the original shares and the bonus shares on a pro rata basis.[5]

3.9 Therefore, if a company was incorporated with a share capital of 100,000 £1 ordinary shares and subsequently issued 50,000 bonus shares fully paid up, any purchase or redemption of less than 50,000 shares will be a distribution in full with no deduction in respect of repayment of share capital. This is regardless of which particular shares have been purchased from any particular shareholder.

3.10 The raison d'être for this provision seems to be that, as the company has not received additional capital for the bonus issue (it represents accumulated and undistributed profits), there should be no reduction for that notional value.

3.11 This prohibition continues until the capitalised profits have been effectively taxed by the disallowance of amounts which would otherwise have been allowed as repayments of share capital. Unfortunately this provision only looks at the transaction from the company's standpoint and therefore creates anomalies for individual shareholders in that the order in which the re-purchases are made can affect individual tax liabilities.

Example

- In 1984 A B C & D incorporate a company with 300,000 £1 ordinary shares fully paid and held equally.
- In 1990 the company capitalises £100,000 of profit and makes a 1 for 3 bonus issue.
- In 1994 A sells 75,000 of his shares to the company for £225,000 in circumstances such that the distribution rules apply.

  Normally an amount equal to the nominal value of the shares sold, (£75,000), would be taken to be a repayment of share capital and the distribution would therefore be £150,000. However, in view of the earlier bonus issue the special rules apply. As the amount of that bonus issue (£100,000) is greater than the amount which would normally be taken as a repayment of share capital (£75,000) no such amounts are allowed until the cumulative amounts disallowed exceed the amount of the earlier bonus issue. In other words, relief for a further £25,000 of nominal value must be disallowed before any amounts can be allowed as repayments of share capital. The distribution in A's case will therefore be £225,000.
- In the following year B also sells 75,000 of his shares for £225,000. Again there would normally be a repayment of share capital of £75,000. However, the first £25,000 of nominal value will be disallowed in order to bring the cumulative disallowance up to the amount of the earlier bonus issue. Once that is done, the remaining £50,000 of nominal value is unaffected by the special rule and is allowed as a repayment of share capital. The distribution in B's case is therefore £175,000.
- If C also sells 75,000 shares for £225,000 in 1996, the distribution will be calculated without regard to s 211 and will only be £150,000.

3.12 Although not specified in the legislation, it would seem that if all three transactions occurred simultaneously, the total distribution would be apportioned amongst the individual shareholders. The moral for shareholders is not to be at the front of the queue.

Bonus issue following earlier purchase or redemption

3.13 Where a company has repaid any share capital, whether by means of a purchase or redemption of own shares or not, and either at the same time, or at some subsequent time, issues fully paid bonus shares, the amount of the bonus share capital will be treated as a distribution.[1] The new shares need not be of the same class as the shares purchased or redeemed.

3.14 This provision operates on a cumulative basis so that the distribution is limited to the amount of share capital repaid, less any previous bonus issues which were treated as a distribution under this provision. It should also be noted that apart from specifying that the repayment of share capital must have taken place after 6 April 1965, this provision applies without a time limit.

3.15 The scope of this provision is restricted where the repaid share capital consisted of fully paid preference shares and which were either in existence on 6 April 1965 or were issued after that date for new consideration.[2] 'New consideration' does not include any which took the form of the surrender of, or a variation of rights in ordinary shares, or which was derived from a repayment of ordinary share capital.

3.16 This provision, which pre-dates the purchase of own shares legislation, was intended to catch situations where a company had repaid some of its share capital and subsequently replenished that capital by capitalising distributable profits and issuing bonus shares. The substance of the transactions would be merely that the shareholders would have received cash which represented distributable profits and the shareholdings would be unchanged.

3.17 If a company purchases, say, 20,000 £1 ordinary shares at £5 per share, and the vendor's circumstances are such that distribution treatment applies, the company will be regarded as making a distribution of £80,000 after allowing for a repayment of capital of £20,000. If at any subsequent time the company were to issue 50,000 fully paid up bonus shares, then a distribution of £20,000 would arise at that time. Because the position is considered solely from the company's viewpoint, it creates inequities amongst the shareholders. The £100,000 sales proceeds may have been received by only one shareholder and between those two points in time the identity of the shareholders may have changed (certainly the vendors of the shares will either no longer be shareholders or will have reduced holdings), so that shareholders who receive the bonus shares will not even have benefited by the receipt of cash.

1 TA 1988 s 210(1).
2 TA 1988 s 210(2).

3.18 Where the earlier purchase or redemption attracted capital treatment, there cannot have been any repayment of capital as the purchase would have been an 'exempt distribution'.[1] As it is possible to engineer distribution treatment for a purchase or redemption if the vendor so wishes, future shareholders may well pay the price for that flexibility.

CAPITAL GAINS TAX POSITION

3.19 Even though the transaction is treated as a distribution and the vendor is assessable to higher rate income tax, he or she has nevertheless made a disposal of the shares for capital gains tax purposes.

3.20 In order to prevent double taxation, the disposal proceeds for capital gains tax purposes are to be reduced by the amounts which fall to be taken into account as the recipient's income for income tax purposes, in other words, the amounts treated as a distribution.[2] Thus in normal cases, the sales proceeds are reduced to the nominal value of the shares sold. Where the special rule mentioned in paragraph **3.6** applies to treat the whole of the sales proceeds as a distribution, the capital gains tax proceeds will be nil. The original cost or March 1982 value is unchanged and therefore a capital loss will arise. Where the nominal value is only partially 'disallowed', a capital loss will only arise to the extent that the cost or March 1982 value is greater than 'allowable' nominal value. The position with regard to corporate vendors is complex and unsatisfactory; this is discussed in detail in Chapter Six.

3.21 If a capital loss arises on a transaction between connected persons,[3] it would only be available to set against gains arising on any future transactions with the company.[4] However, for this restriction to apply there must be both a disposal and an acquisition. Although this matter is not beyond academic debate, the Revenue accept that the company does not acquire the shares on a purchase and thus the restriction on the use of the relief does not apply to the loss arising on a purchase or redemption.[5] The basis for this view is that company law requires the shares to be cancelled on completion and as a result there is no asset which can be acquired.

---

1 TA 1988 s 219(1), therefore outside s 210.
2 TCGA 1992 s 37(1).
3 TCGA 1992 s 18(1).
4 TCGA 1992 s 18(3).
5 Inland Revenue Capital Gains Manual CG 58602.

Chapter Four

TAXATION: CAPITAL TREATMENT

4.1 The relief introduced by FA 1982 provides for a purchase or redemption of its own shares by a company to be accorded 'exempt distribution' status, provided certain conditions are fulfilled. As a result a transaction which qualifies for this status does not give rise to advance corporation tax or higher rate income tax liabilities. Instead the vendor becomes liable to capital gains tax based upon the full amount of the sales proceeds. There are two scenarios in which exempt distribution status may apply:

1 purchases for the benefit of a trade;[1] and
2 purchases to fund an inheritance tax liability.[2]

PURCHASES FOR THE BENEFIT OF A TRADE

4.2 This type of transaction is plagued by numerous tests, all of which need to be satisfied, and each of which will be considered in turn.

The status test

4.3 The shareholder, and any nominee in whose name the shares are held, must be both resident and ordinarily resident in the UK in the year of assessment in which the purchase takes place. The purpose of this test is fairly clear in the case of the owner of the shares. If he or she were not resident and not ordinarily resident in the UK, then no capital gains tax liability would arise on the sale of the shares, whereas if the distribution treatment applied this would give rise to income liable to UK income tax, subject, of course, to any relief available under any appropriate Double Tax Agreement (DTA).

4.4 It is, however, less clear to see why the residence status of a nominee should be of any consequence. After all, it is the residence status of the beneficial owner of the shares which would determine the exposure to UK tax in

1 TA 1988 s 219(1)(a).
2 TA 1988 s 219(1)(b).

the normal course of events. Perhaps the objective was to prevent a non-resident and non-ordinarily resident shareholder from transferring shares to a resident and ordinarily resident nominee prior to a purchase or redemption, or perhaps it was included as a deliberate means of escape from capital treatment. As will be seen later, it is possible to fail this test deliberately by transferring shares to a non-resident and/or non-ordinarily resident nominee.

4.5 The one instance where the actual residence status of the shareholder is ignored is in the case of personal representatives, whose status is taken to be the same as the deceased's immediately before his or her death.[1]

The ownership test

4.6 The vendor must have owned the shares being sold throughout the five years ending with the purchase.[2] References to the owner of shares are to the beneficial owner of the shares, the exceptions being where shares are held in trust (other than on bare trusts) or are held by personal representatives, in which cases they are regarded as the owners.[3]

4.7 The required length of ownership is relaxed to take into account previous ownership by a spouse, provided the vendor and the spouse were living together at the time of the transfer and, if that spouse is still alive, they are still living together at the date of the purchase of the shares by the company.[4] Permanent separation or divorce occurring after the transfer of the shares but before the purchase by the company would negate the relief, unless the transferor spouse had died before the date of the purchase.

4.8 A further relaxation occurs where the vendor becomes entitled to the shares under a will or intestacy, or where he or she is the personal representative of a deceased shareholder. In such a case, the ownership requirement is only three years and the previous ownership by the deceased is taken into account.[5]

4.9 Where the vendor has acquired shares at different times and has held some for less than the required period, only those proceeds relating to the shares held for that period will attract capital treatment, the balance being treated as a distribution. If the company were to purchase only some of the shares then the question of identification arises. Shares sold are identified with those acquired at an earlier rather than at a later date, ie on a 'first in, first out' basis. However, where the shareholder has previously disposed of shares of the same class, those earlier disposals are to be regarded as having been made out of later acquisitions in preference to earlier ones.[6] The effect of this is to identify the shares being purchased with those held longest,

1 TA 1988 s 220(3).
2 TA 1988 s 220(5).
3 TA 1988 s 229(2).
4 TA 1988 s 220(6).
5 TA 1988 s 220(7).
6 TA 1988 s 220(8).

which is the most advantageous method for the shareholder, assuming of course, that capital treatment is desirable.

4.10 If, within the five years preceding the purchase by the company, there has been a reorganisation of the share capital, eg bonus issues or share exchanges, and for capital gains tax purposes the current shares are regarded as having been acquired at the date of acquisition of the original shares in respect of which they were issued, then for capital treatment purposes the current shares are also regarded as having been acquired on that earlier date.[1] This relaxation however, does not, apply in the case of rights issues or stock dividends.

4.11 The five-year period is rather harsh when compared to business property relief for inheritance tax where the requirement is only two years' ownership. The period may have been chosen to prevent equity investors realising their investment in this manner. However, given that there is an overriding need to show that the purchase is for the benefit of a trade, this ownership requirement seems to be an example of Revenue overkill. If a trade is being disadvantaged by the presence of a dissident shareholder, then it must continue being disadvantaged until that person has been a shareholder for five years before the company can make an exempt distribution to get rid of him or her.

The trading benefit test

4.12 This is one of the fundamental tests by which purchases stand or fall. The purchase must be undertaken wholly or mainly for the purpose of benefiting a trade being carried on by the company or any of its 75% subsidiaries. In addition it must not form part of a scheme or arrangement, the main purpose, or one of the main purposes, of which is either the avoidance of tax or to enable the owner of the shares to participate in the profits of the company without receiving a dividend.[2]

4.13 From this requirement it follows that:

1 fairly obviously, there must be a trade. Therefore capital treatment can never be afforded to the purchase of shares by a company which carries on activities which do not amount to a 'trade'. The most obvious example is, perhaps, a property investment company. Certain activities which are trades are, nevertheless, treated as not being trades for this purpose. These are the usual ones of dealing in shares, securities, land or futures;[3]
2 the trade must be currently carried on. Capital treatment will not be granted if the trade concerned has already been discontinued or indeed if it has not yet commenced;
3 in order to show that the purchase of shares from a shareholder will lead to a trading benefit, it is generally necessary to demonstrate that the

1 TA 1988 s 220(9).
2 TA 1988 s 219(1)(a).
3 TA 1988 s 229(1).

continuing presence of the vendor is having some detrimental effect on the company's trade. In the case of private companies, where the vendor shareholder is also a director, a boardroom disagreement over the management of the company or future plans will clearly have such a detrimental effect.

The Revenue, however, go much further than that and accept that the retention of any unwilling shareholder can be prejudicial to the trade. They quote as examples a founder shareholder/director wishing to stand down to make way for new management and the legatees of a deceased shareholder who have no wish to be involved with the company.[1]

Where the purpose is to buy out a dissident shareholder, Revenue practice is to expect that dissident to dispose of all his or her shares and resign as a director. Indeed it would be difficult to see how the trade could benefit from the purchase if the dissident were still involved with the management of the company.

It may be that the company does not have sufficient resources available to buy the whole of the shares at once. In these circumstances the Revenue will allow a partial purchase provided the company has the intention to purchase the remaining shares when further finance becomes available. Although this would enable the trading benefit test to be satisfied, the substantial reduction and connection tests mentioned below could still prove a problem.

4 the advantage arising or which can be expected to arise from the purchase must be for the benefit of the trade and not just for the benefit of the company, although in most cases this will be the same thing.

The question of the trading benefit test is discussed in more detail in Chapter Eight.

The connection test

4.14 A further reason why a vendor should sell the entire shareholding is to satisfy the requirement that, immediately after the purchase, he or she is not 'connected' with the purchasing company or with any other company which is a member of the same group.[2]

4.15 For these purposes a person is connected if he or she possesses, directly or indirectly, or is entitled to acquire more than 30% of either:

1 the issued ordinary share capital;
2 the loan capital and issued share capital (of any class);
3 the voting rights; or
4 the assets available for distribution to equity holders in the event of a winding up or in any other circumstances.[3]

---

1 Statement of Practice SP2/82.
2 TA 1988 s 223(1).
3 TA 1988 s 228(2) and (4)

Loans made by persons in the ordinary course of their business which includes the lending of money, and who take no part in the management or conduct of the company, are ignored for this purpose.[1]

4.16 In looking at a person's rights in the company he or she is assumed to have the rights of his or her associates,[2] which are defined[3] as:

1 his or her spouse and minor children;
2 his or her parents (but only in the case of a person under the age of 18);
3 a company with which he or she is connected, and any other company under the control of the first company;
4 the trustees, other than bare trustees, of any settlement of which the person is the settlor or for which he or she has indirectly provided property or has made a reciprocal agreement for someone else to do so;
5 the trustees of any settlement under which he or she may become entitled to more than a 5% interest in the company shares held by the trustees; and
6 the personal representatives of a deceased shareholder where the person is entitled to more than a 5% interest in the shares held by the deceased.

4.17 In all cases the individual is an associate of the associates themselves. Additionally, a company which is under the control of an individual is an associate of any company with which that individual is connected, but not, apparently, vice versa.[4] Just to ensure that all possibilities have been covered, it is provided that where one person is 'accustomed to act on the directions of another' in relation to the company's affairs, those persons will be each other's associates.[5]

4.18 The reference to the trustees of a settlement does not apply to situations where shares are held on trust as part of an exempt approved pension scheme or for the benefit of the employees of the purchasing company (or a member of the same group) or their dependants.[6]

4.19 The main purpose behind the connection test is to counter any attempts to claim capital treatment where the vendor retains a significant interest in the company. This would be via the medium of his or her close family or bodies of persons who might be expected to act in accordance with his or her wishes.

4.20 This is an understandable concern but the test can create significant problems for the private company. For example, where the whole of the issued shares are held by a married couple, there can never be capital treatment for a purchase of own shares as the vendor will always be connected with the company by means of the shareholding of the spouse. What is needed in this situation is a third shareholder who is not an associate. This could be an adult son or daughter who has acquired shares before the purchase of own shares takes place.

---

1 TA 1988 s 223(3).
2 TA 1988 s 228(8).
3 TA 1988 s 227.
4 TA 1988 s 227(4).
5 TA 1988 s 227(7).
6 TA 1988 s 227(8).

4.21 Additionally this test creates problems where the company may not have the necessary funds available to pay for the shares in full and it is necessary for the vendor to lend some or all of the proceeds back to the company. By so doing he or she might end up being entitled to more than 30% of the combined share and loan capital and fail to satisfy the test.

4.22 Although the test is to be applied 'immediately after' the purchase, any thoughts of arranging for a vendor to be unconnected for a time following the purchase, but for him or her to acquire a greater interest in the company at a later date, need to be re-examined. A further condition to be satisfied is that the purchase must not be part of any scheme or arrangement which is designed or is 'likely' to result in the vendor or any associate having interests in the company which would breach the connection test if those interests had been in existence immediately after the purchase.[1] Furthermore, any transaction, whether planned or not, which occurs within one year after the purchase is automatically regarded as part of such a scheme.[2]

4.23 This latter condition is particularly harsh as the vendor is hostage to the actions of his or her associates. If one of those were to acquire a further interest in the company, or another group member, within that period, the test could cease to be satisfied. Whilst tax legislation assumes that an individual would control the actions of his or her associates or that, at the very least, they would act in concert, this cosy state of affairs does not always exist in real life.

The substantial reduction test

4.24 By its very nature this test is only of relevance if the vendor still retains a shareholding in the company immediately following the purchase. In such a case the vendor's interest must have been 'substantially reduced' as a result of the purchase.[3] In common with the connection test, the interests of any associates[4] are also taken into account.[5] Thus it is the combined interests of the vendor and his or her associates which must be substantially reduced.[6]

4.25 If the purchasing company is a member of a group of companies and, immediately after the purchase, the vendor either:

1 holds shares in other group companies; or
2 continues to hold some shares in the purchasing company and, immediately before the purchase, held some shares in another group member,

then the combined interests in the group of the vendor and his or her associates must be substantially reduced.

1 TA 1988 s 223(2).
2 TA 1988 s 223(3).
3 TA 1988 s 221(1).
4 See para 4.16 .
5 TA 1988 s 221(3).
6 TA 1988 s 221(2).

4.26 A group for these purposes comprises a parent company and its 51% subsidiaries where that parent is not also a 51% subsidiary of another company.[1] The definition of a group is extended, for these purposes only, to include any company which, within the three years prior to the purchase, began to carry on a business previously carried on by either the purchasing company or another group member.[2] The use of the word 'business' rather than 'trade' means that this can include the holding of shares. In addition, a company which had previously ceased to be a 51% subsidiary will be treated as remaining within the group, if, at the time of the purchase, arrangements exist whereby it could become a subsidiary again.[3]

4.27 The object behind these provisions is to prevent advance fragmentation of a group with a view to circumventing the substantial reduction test. However, as their application does not depend upon the existence of a tax avoidance motive, they will be triggered by perfectly normal commercial transactions and may provide an unpleasant surprise for vendors.

Nominal value

4.28 The test requires the nominal value of the combined shareholding immediately after the purchase to be less than 75% of the nominal value of the combined holding prior to that purchase.[4] In other words, the reduction must be more than 25%.

4.29 Because the purchased shares are cancelled and the company's issued share capital reduced accordingly, it is not sufficient for a vendor simply to sell 25% of his or her shareholding. In a straightforward case of one vendor selling ordinary shares, the amount required to be sold to satisfy the substantial reduction test can be found by applying the formula:

$$\frac{S \times C}{4C - 3S}$$

where S = the shareholding of the vendor before the purchase, and C = the company's issued share capital before the purchase.

4.30 This can be illustrated by the following example:

Example

Henry holds 550 out of 1,000 shares in issue and none of the other shareholders are his associates. He must sell at least 235 shares to achieve a substantial reduction, ie

$$\frac{550 \times 1{,}000}{4{,}000 - 1{,}650} = \frac{550{,}000}{2{,}350} = 234.042\text{, rounded up to } 235$$

His shareholding would then become 315 out of a reduced issued share capital of 765, a holding of 41% which is a reduction of 25.5%.

1 TA 1988 s 222(9).
2 TA 1988 s 222(10) and (11).
3 TA 1988 s 222(12).
4 TA 1988 s 221(4).

However, if his wife, Minnie, held 150 shares prior to the purchase, then Henry would be regarded as having a 70% interest and consequently would have to sell 369 shares to satisfy the test, ie:

$$\frac{700 \times 1{,}000}{4{,}000 - 2{,}100} = \frac{700{,}000}{1{,}900} = 368.421\text{, rounded up to } 369$$

Suppose, however, that instead of Henry selling, Minnie wanted to sell 100 of her shares. In order to satisfy that test a total of 369 shares would still have to be sold, calculated as above, so that this would require Henry to sell 269 shares of his own at the same time.

In such a situation, where an associate agrees to sell some of his or her shares in order to allow another person to satisfy the substantial reduction test, that associate is not required to satisfy either that test or the connection test in order to qualify for capital treatment on their own disposal.[1]

4.31 In a group situation, the vendor's interest in the share capital is measured by taking the fraction of his or her holding of each company's nominal share capital, adding those fractions together and dividing that answer by the number of companies in which he or she holds or, prior to the purchase, has held shares.[2] The effect is to take an average of the vendor's percentage shareholdings.

Example

If an individual holds 25% of the share capital of Company A and 40% of Company B, his interest in the group, prior to any purchase is (25+40)/2 = 32.5%. If Company B were to purchase his entire shareholding, his interest in the group would then become (25+0)/2 = 12.5%.

Distributable profits

4.32 It is also required that the vendor's entitlement to share in the profits available for distribution, immediately after the purchase or redemption, be less than 75% of his or her previous entitlement.

4.33 This requirement covers situations where the nominal value is not a true indication of a person's interest in the share capital of a company. It also, no doubt, exists to block attempts to circumvent the nominal value requirement.

4.34 In applying this requirement, the profits available for distribution are those computed for the purposes of the Companies Act[3] with the addition of certain amounts:[4]

1 in all cases the sum of £100. This blanket addition is intended to cover the position where a company would not otherwise have any distributable

1 TA 1988 s 224.
2 TA 1988 s 222(5).
3 See para 2.9.
4 TA 1988 s 221(7).

profits upon which this requirement could be based, it being generally accepted that a company with a deficit on its revenue reserves does not have a negative figure of distributable profits, it simply has none at all. Therefore the effect of this addition will be to give all companies a minimum figure of distributable profits of £100;

2 in any case where a person is entitled to a periodic fixed rate or fixed amount of distribution, the maximum amount of that distribution to which he or she would be entitled for a year. This would cover the situations where a cumulative preference dividend was unpaid for lack of distributable profits. The shareholder concerned would similarly be deemed to be entitled to that same amount in applying this requirement; and

3 the amount of any excess of the purchase or redemption price over the profits available for distribution. This therefore equates to the 'permitted capital sum' in purchases out of capital[1] and the proceeds of any new share issue used to fund the purchase. The reference to profits available for distribution presumably refers to the 'real' distributable profits under the Companies Act, not the notional distributable profits which are the object of this calculation.

Example

A company which was incorporated in 1985 has an issued share capital of 100,000 £1 ordinary shares and 7,500 10% preference shares. Dennis owns 20,000 ordinary shares and the whole of the preference shares. Assuming that he has no associates and that the company purchases 9,000 of his ordinary shares for £5,000, he will satisfy the substantial reduction test in terms of nominal value, ie applying the formula at paragraph **4.29**, the minimum number of shares he would have to sell would be:

$$\frac{27{,}500 \times 107{,}500}{430{,}000 - 82{,}500} = \frac{2{,}956{,}250{,}000}{347{,}500} = 8{,}507.19\text{, rounded up to } 8{,}508$$

However, whether he satisfies the additional requirement will be determined by the level of the company's distributable profits and the purchase price of the shares. If those profits at the date of the purchase were £10,000, the profits available for distribution would be calculated as:

Distributable profits	10,000
Statutory addition	100
Preference dividend	750
	10,850

Dennis's entitlement prior to the purchase is

Preference dividend	750
20% of balance of 10,100	2,020
	2,770

which represents 25.53% of the total.

1 See para 2.30.

After the purchase his entitlement is

Preference dividend	750
12.08%[1] of the balance of £10,100	1,220
	1,970

which represents 18.16% of the total, and is a reduction of 28.87%. The requirement would therefore be satisfied.

However, if the company had no distributable profits, and consequently the purchase were made wholly out of capital, then the profits available for distribution become:

Distributable profits	0
Statutory addition	100
Preference dividend	750
excess of purchase price over profits	5,000
	5,850

Dennis's entitlement prior to the purchase in that case would have been:

Preference dividend	750
20% of balance of 5,100	1,020
	1,770

which represents 30.26% of the total.

After the purchase his entitlement would become

Preference dividend	750
12.08% of balance of £5,100	616
	1,366

which represents 23.35% of the total, and is a reduction of only 22.8%. The requirement would therefore not be satisfied even though the required reduction has been achieved in terms of nominal value.

4.35 In a group context, the vendor's entitlement to the profits available for distribution is measured by reference to his or her entitlement to the profits of all group members.[2] The problem faced by the vendor is that, because each company will have differing amounts of distributable profits, those amounts will affect the vendor's chances of satisfying the requirement.

Example

A Ltd and B Ltd are members of the same group of companies. Harry holds 10% of the ordinary share capital of A Ltd which has distributable profits of £225,000. He also holds 35% of the share capital of B Ltd which has distributable profits of £20,000. B Ltd purchases Harry's entire shareholding and funds the cost out of an issue of new shares.

1 11,000 ordinary shares out of 91,000 in issue.
2 TA 1988 s 222(7).

In terms of nominal value, Harry's interest will have been reduced from (10+35)/2 = 22.5% to (10+0)/2 = 5%, a reduction of over 77%, therefore, on that basis, there has been a substantial reduction.

However, in terms of the profits available for distribution, Harry's interest prior to the purchase was:

A Ltd 10% × £225,100	22,510
B Ltd 35% × £20,100	7,035
	29,545

After the purchase that interest is reduced by the entitlement to a share in the profits of B Ltd, £7,035. This is a reduction of only 23%, consequently the requirement is not met and capital treatment will not be available for the purchase.

4.36 The following example can also be used:

Assuming the same facts as in the previous example but in this case the distributable profits of A Ltd are only £200,000. Harry's interest prior to the purchase would have been:

A Ltd 10% × £200,100	20,010
B Ltd 35% × £20,100	7,035
	27,045

The reduction would again be £7,035 but this time the percentage reduction would be 26% and the requirement would be satisfied.

The company status test

4.37 The purchasing company must be an unquoted trading company or the unquoted holding company of a trading group.[1] A unquoted company is one which has none of its shares quoted in the official list of a stock exchange, or which is not a 51% subsidiary of a company any of whose shares are so quoted.[2] The Alternative Investment Market (AIM) is not regarded as an official list of a stock exchange for these purposes.[3]

4.38 There is no specific requirement that the purchasing company be incorporated in the UK. It would, however, need to be within the charge to UK corporation tax by virtue of its residence. If the company was not resident the distribution rules would not be applicable and capital treatment would not be available. In such a case the vendor would be assessable under Sch D, case V.

4.39 When a company incorporated outside the UK is resident here for tax purposes as a result of the location of its central management and control, it will not be subject to UK company law, at least in respect of any purchase of its shares. The law of the country of incorporation will determine whether a purchase or redemption of its own shares is possible.

1 TA 1988 s 219(1).
2 TA 1988 s 229(1).
3 Inland Revenue Press Release 20 February 1995 (see also Statement of Practice SP18/80 in conection with the Unlisted Securities Market which closed in December 1996).

PURCHASES TO FUND INHERITANCE TAX LIABILITIES

4.40 Alternative grounds for capital treatment arise where the sale is taking place for the purpose of raising funds to pay an inheritance tax liability arising on a death.[1] To qualify under this head the company must satisfy the status test and in addition:

1 the inheritance tax must be the liability of 'the person to whom the payment is made', presumably the vendor shareholder, and be charged on a death;
2 the whole or substantially the whole of the sales proceeds, less any amount needed to pay any capital gains tax on the sale, must be used to pay the inheritance tax within two years of the death; and
3 the payment of the inheritance tax could not have been made by means of methods other than the purchase or redemption without 'undue hardship'.

4.41 The tests mentioned earlier in the case of a purchase for the benefit of a trade, ie residence of vendor, period of ownership, substantial reduction and connection tests do not apply in the case of a claim under this head.

4.42 The conditions in paragraph **4.40** above give rise to a number of comments. Firstly, whilst it is fairly clear that capital treatment will be applicable where the inheritance tax is charged on the death of a shareholder, the question arises as to whether such treatment can also be applied where the death was of someone who was not a shareholder. Such a situation may arise where an individual had made a significant lifetime gift to a shareholder and subsequently died within seven years.

4.43 The Capital Taxes Office are understood to hold the view that inheritance tax arising on a potentially exempt transfer made less than seven years before the donor's death does not satisfy the necessary condition. This view seems to have no basis in law. The phrase 'charged on a death' does not simply mean charged on an estate passing on a death, but also, surely, 'charged as a consequence of a death'. Unless and until the donor dies within the seven year period, any lifetime transfer which is a potentially exempt transfer[2] is totally exempt; it is a non-event as far as inheritance tax is concerned. It is the death of the donor that creates the charge to tax and that tax is the liability of the donee.[3] Therefore the tax is 'charged on a death' and it is the liability of the person to whom the payment (ie the purchase or redemption price) is made.

4.44 A further point is that the liability need not arise on the shares themselves. Indeed, with 100% business property relief currently available on all

1 TA 1988 s 219(1)(b).
2 This is a misnomer. These transfers are 'potentially chargeable' or 'provisionally exempt'.
3 IHTA 1984 ss 199(1)(a) and 204.

holdings of unquoted shares in trading companies, such a liability is unlikely to arise unless relief is denied because of 'excepted assets'[1] or because the ownership requirement[2] has not been satisfied.

4.45 The parliamentary draftsman clearly intended shareholders to suffer some hardship, so long as it was not 'undue' hardship. There is no published guidance and the onus seems to be very much on the shareholder to present a detailed argument to the Revenue. In Statement of Practice SP2/82 they advise submitting 'a full explanation of the circumstances in which there would be "undue hardship" if the tax liability were to be discharged otherwise than through the purchase of own shares from this or any other such company.'

4.46 Revenue policy seems to be to consider the resources currently available to the claimant, and any further action he or she could take to increase those resources to enable the tax to be paid. Thus it has been stated that where the company has distributable profits sufficient to discharge the inheritance tax liability and the shareholder has a controlling interest, the Revenue would refuse capital treatment on the grounds that he could use his voting power to vote himself dividends out of which the tax could be paid.[3]

4.47 This policy of looking at the other resources available and what other steps the taxpayer could take, is in marked contrast to the Revenue's policy in respect of capital gains tax prior to 1996/97. Before 6 April 1996, where the consideration for a disposal was payable in instalments over a period exceeding 18 months, and the taxpayer could show that to pay the tax in one sum he would suffer 'undue hardship', the tax could itself be paid by instalments.[4] The Revenue's approach to 'undue hardship' was explained when the original legislation, introduced in the 1972 Finance Bill, was being debated at committee stage:

> 'In considering whether undue hardship would arise, the Revenue would look primarily to the question whether the vendor or disponer could reasonably be expected to pay the tax on the full amount immediately, in the light of the resources made available by the particular transaction involved. Regard would not normally be paid to the other resources of the taxpayer if it could be shown that the instalment arrangement was in the circumstances, and apart from any tax considerations, a normal commercial arrangement and reflected a genuine deferment of the enjoyment of the consideration. The Revenue practice would, of course, be kept under review, in the light of its effect on actual cases arising.'[5]

4.48 This does beg the question as to why, for capital gains tax, regard was not normally paid to the taxpayer's other resources whereas it seems to be automatic in the case of inheritance tax. Is hardship created by capital gains tax any more 'undue' than that created by inheritance tax?

---

1 IHTA 1984 s 112.
2 IHTA 1984 s 109.
3 Hansard Vol 494 Col 1349 17 March 1988.
4 TCGA 1992 s 280. The requirement for 'undue hardship' was removed with effect from 6 April 1996 (1 April 1996 for companies).
5 Official Report, Standing Committee E, Cols 1358–1359, 22 June 1972.

4.49 In deciding whether the payment of inheritance tax will create undue hardship, account must be taken of the extent to which that tax may qualify to be paid by 10 equal annual instalments.[1] Obviously the opportunity to claim instalment relief on any tax due on land, shares and businesses (where 100% business or agricultural property relief is not due) will be a factor that will work against any hardship claim. It also needs to be remembered that relief will only be available in respect of amounts used to pay tax within two years of the death.

4.50 A curious feature of this route to capital treatment is that no formal claims procedure is prescribed. The draftsman may well have considered that an advance clearance was so akin to a claim that no separate claims procedure was required. If a vendor is likely to suffer 'undue hardship' then a clearance application should be submitted before the transaction takes place, if only to ensure that the vendor does not end up in greater hardship because tax is charged under the distribution treatment. In addition, the company has to notify the Inspector of all purchases which have not been treated as a distribution and the reasons for that treatment; this, again, is a 'quasi-claim'.

4.51 This line of approach is understandable but does not recognise that a clearance application is not mandatory. It is just conceivable that a purchase goes ahead without a clearance and the company overlooks the reporting requirement. When the position finally comes to the attention of the Inspector, there would seem to be no reason, apart from the Inspector's natural suspicion, why capital treatment should not be given, provided that 'undue hardship' can be established and, more importantly, that the proceeds were used to pay the inheritance tax within the prescribed two years of purchase.

ADVANCE CLEARANCES

4.52 In view of the subjective nature of the trading benefit test, it is fortunate that the legislation provides for an advance clearance procedure. A unique feature of this procedure is that the Board of Inland Revenue can be required to confirm that a proposed transaction either does or does not qualify for capital treatment. It should be appreciated that the advance clearance procedure is not obligatory, merely advisable.

4.53 Despite the fact that most of the tests which need to be satisfied to enable capital treatment to apply relate to the vendor, the application is required to be made by the company. This in itself is unlikely to cause any problem as a vendor would make it a condition of the purchase that the company had obtained the appropriate clearance.

4.54 The Board have to notify their decision within 30 days of the application unless they serve a notice within that time requiring further information. In the latter case their decision must be notified within 30 days of receipt of

1 IHTA 1984 s 227.

that further information (unless, of course, the Board serve another notice requiring even more information).

4.55 Because of this ability of the Board to call for further information, it obviously makes sense to try and avoid such situations arising. The original application should contain all the information likely to be required by the Board and in particular, care should be taken to explain why the purchase will benefit the trade or why undue hardship will arise. Time spent in refining the clearance application will be worthwhile in the long term, if only because the resulting decision will be void if the application does not fully and accurately disclose all material facts and circumstances.

4.56 The Revenue's internal instructions advise local Inspectors that if they receive a clearance application in error, they should return it to the applicant and tell them to re-submit it to Taxes Registry, Bush House in London. However, Inspectors are then told to send a copy of the application to Company Tax Division 2 at Somerset House.[1] It seems rather pointless that the applicant should have to re-submit the application to Bush House, whence it will end up in Somerset House, when a copy will already have arrived at Somerset House from the Inspector. What this does mean is that if, after submitting the application to the local office, the applicant has second thoughts and either decides not to proceed or to amend its contents, the original version will already be on the Revenue's files.

4.57 A guide to the format of clearance applications is contained in Statement of Practice SP2/82 which is reproduced at Appendix 1. It is important to note that the Revenue wish to know 'details of any other transactions between the company and the vendor at or about the same time'. This requirement is intended to flush out such items as ex gratia payments, pension contributions and other collateral transactions. When and if clearance is given for capital treatment, it will usually be couched in the following terms:

> 'On the basis of the information supplied, and provided that no payments or assets have or are intended to be made or passed to the vendor except as already notified to me, the Board are satisfied that the provisions of Section 219 Income and Corporation Taxes Act 1988 will apply to the payment to be made in respect of the shares'.

It is obviously extremely important that any transactions with the vendor should be disclosed in the clearance application. The Revenue's attitude to collateral transactions is considered in Chapter Ten.

REPORTING REQUIREMENTS

4.58 These requirements impose four obligations:[2]

1 where a company purchases or redeems its own shares and does not treat

---

1 Inland Revenue Company Tax Manual CT 1757.
2 TA 1988 s 226.

the payment as a distribution, it must report details of the payment to the Inspector within 60 days and give the reasons why it is believed that the payment is an exempt distribution. Obviously in the normal course of events, clearance will have been received and it will only be necessary to refer the Inspector to that fact and quote the reference under which it was received.

If an Inspector receives a notification of a purchase or redemption which has not been treated as a distribution, and for which he has not been informed of any clearance granted for capital treatment, he is required to submit an immediate report to Company Tax Division 2.[1] It may be that the first question the Revenue will ask the company is why it did not seek advance clearance;

2 in the case of a purchase intended to benefit the trade, any person 'connected' with the company (as previously defined) who knows of any 'scheme or arrangement' has to give notice to the Inspector within 60 days of becoming aware of both the payment and the scheme, giving particulars of that scheme. This is aimed at schemes which are intended to allow the vendor or any associate to obtain interests in any company, which if they had existed immediately after the purchase would have breached the connection test.

It is difficult to see that anyone in that position would actually invite Revenue attention by making such a return. The main effect of this provision will be to enable the Revenue to invoke penalties[2] in suitable cases;

3 where there has been a payment to which capital treatment has been applied because the purchase was intended to benefit the trade, and the Inspector has reason to believe that either:

(a) a scheme exists which is designed to thwart the connection test, as mentioned above;
(b) there is a scheme designed to enable the owner of the shares to participate in the profits of the company without receiving a dividend; or
(c) there is a scheme for the avoidance of tax;

he may serve a notice on the company, or any person connected to the company, to supply him, within 60 days, with a declaration stating whether or not such a scheme exists and any other information he may reasonably require;

4 where the purchase has been treated as an exempt distribution, the vendor can be required by the Inspector to state whether the payment was received on behalf of any person, and if so to state that person's name and address.

4.59 Failure to furnish the required information or the fraudulent or negligent furnishing of incorrect information can give rise to penalties.

4.60 No time limit is specified by which the Inspector must issue any notices under (3) or (4). It is therefore possible, and indeed very probable, that any such notices would be issued some considerable time after the purchase or

---

1 Inland Revenue Company Tax Manual CT 1757.
2 TMA 1970 s 98.

redemption, when perhaps material facts which were not made available to Somerset House later come to light.

CONCLUSION

4.61 Whether capital treatment will be beneficial or not will depend upon individual circumstances. Those vendors entitled to retirement relief or re-investment relief or with a high base cost or March 1982 value will benefit, but others, including trustees of life interest or discretionary trusts and those with a low base cost may prefer distribution treatment. In those circumstances, steps may have to be taken to deliberately breach the conditions for capital treatment. A discussion of whether capital treatment is desirable in particular cases can be found in Chapter Six, whilst possible steps to avoid capital treatment are discussed in Chapter Seven.

Chapter Five

TAXATION: THE ASSOCIATED COSTS

THE STAMP DUTY

Purchases

5.1 Despite the fact that both company law and direct tax law seek to assist companies to purchase their own shares, subject to certain restrictions, it is rather surprising that there is currently no relief from stamp duty, although it seems that one was intended. In a reply to a parliamentary question in 1984 the Financial Secretary to the Treasury stated:

> 'The Companies Act 1981 enables companies to purchase their own shares. A specific exemption from ad valorem stamp duty was not provided although it was intended that s 52 of the Act[1] (Disclosure of Particulars of Purchase and Authorised Contracts) should effectively provide for this. Doubts have arisen as to whether s 52 achieved this objective.'
>
> Ad valorem duty is payable on any conveyance or transfer on sale and [Stamp Act] 1891 s 54 provides that the expression 'conveyance on sale' includes every instrument whereby any property sold is transferred or vested in the purchaser. The Revenue are advised that although the matter is not free from doubt there are grounds for holding that this section does not apply when a company purchases its own shares. This is the view that the Board proposes to adopt. A Secretary or Registrar of a company may accordingly amend the register without requiring that any delivery statement is stamped with ad valorem duty.'[2]

5.2 Looking at the successor to s 52, it is not immediately apparent how that could be said to have effectively provided for a stamp duty exemption. It seems CA 1981 was amended on its passage through Parliament in an attempt to remove the need for a document which would attract duty, and clearly failed.

5.3 It has been suggested that a stock transfer form should always be submitted to the Stamp Office, referring to the Press Release and asking for the transfer to be stamped to denote that it is not chargeable with duty.[3]

---

1 Now CA 1985 s 169.
2 Inland Revenue Press Release 1 May 1984.
3 Stamp Act 1891 s 12(3).

5.4 However, is a stock transfer form really needed? The question turns upon whether it is believed that the purchased shares cease to exist on completion or whether they need to be transferred to the company and continue to exist for some scintilla of time until cancellation. If a transfer is not required, then there is no instrument to attract duty, but if a transfer is needed, is it safe to register that share transfer without it having been duly stamped,[1] even if that is merely denoting that it is not chargeable with duty? Such a debate is no doubt very absorbing but in the practical world in which most practitioners operate, it is an unnecessary luxury. The Press Release is a clear statement of practice from the taxing authority upon which taxpayers should be able to rely.

5.5 For reasons which are also not readily apparent, the advent of the 'Big Bang' in the Stock Exchange led to the demise of the stamp duty exemption when an ad valorem charge on Form 169 was introduced.[2] This is the return which must be submitted to the Registrar of Companies within 28 days of purchase. The return is to be 'treated for all purposes of the Stamp Act 1891, as if it were an instrument transferring the shares on sale to the company in pursuance of the contract'.[3] As a result the return is treated as a 'conveyance or transfer on sale' and duty is levied at 50p on every £100 or part thereof of the purchase price.[4]

5.6 Where the purchase would otherwise attract any relief from duty, does that relief still apply? For example, if a subsidiary company were to purchase some of its own shares from its parent company, would this attract associated companies relief?[5] This gives relief from duty on a 'conveyance or transfer on sale' where the effect of the instrument is to convey or transfer a beneficial interest in property from one company to another, where the two are 'associated'. In this context companies are associated if one is a 75% subsidiary of the other or both are 75% subsidiaries of a third company.

5.7 At first sight the relief may be thought to be available, but as it is generally accepted that a purchase of own shares does not involve a transfer of property, this would prevent associated companies relief from applying. A further stumbling block exists in the anti-avoidance provisions[6] which deny relief if, inter alia, the transaction is part of a series of transactions whereby the necessary 75% relationship is broken by a reduction in the shares held in the subsidiary by the parent.

Redemptions

5.8 The position here is without controversy. The shares being redeemed cease to exist at the point of redemption and there cannot be any transfer to

1 Stamp Act 1891 s 17 imposes a penalty of £10 on a company secretary or registrar who registers an instrument which is not 'duly stamped'.
2 FA 1986 s 66.
3 FA 1986 s 66(2).
4 FA 1963 s 55(1A).
5 FA 1930 s 42.
6 FA 1967 s 27(3).

the company. There is therefore no requirement for a stock transfer form and no instrument which could attract stamp duty. The return required under the Companies Act on Form 169 is specifically only for purchases. In the case of a redemption, a return is required on Form 122, but it is not dutiable.

STAMP DUTY RESERVE TAX

5.9 Once again, whether such a charge applies to a purchase of own shares depends upon whether it is considered that there is a transfer of property. A liability to stamp duty reserve tax can only arise if there is an agreement to transfer chargeable securities for a consideration in money or monies worth.[1] This charge arises on the expiry of two months from the date the agreement is made unless an instrument of transfer is executed and is duly stamped with the appropriate duty or otherwise is required to be stamped.[2]

5.10 As mentioned earlier, the Revenue's view is that no property is being transferred and consequently no stamp duty reserve tax can arise. However, those wishing to cover all options can submit a stock transfer form for adjudication, as mentioned in paragraph **5.3**, and that will satisfy the requirement for exemption.

PROFESSIONAL COSTS

The company's position

5.11 It is tempting, logical and dangerous to assume that if a purchase of own shares has been accepted by the Revenue as being undertaken to benefit a trade, the costs involved would be allowable as deductions in arriving at the company's taxable profits.

5.12 The Revenue's internal instructions[3] advise Inspectors that legal costs are 'generally' disallowable on the grounds that they are capital expenditure.[4] In 1991 they went on record as follows:

> 'Legal (or other) expenditure incurred by a trading company on the redemption, repayment or purchase of its own shares is considered to be capital expenditure, either on general principles or by reference to TA 1988 s 74(f) (deduction for capital not allowable). It is capital expenditure on general principles because it is part of the cost of changing the share capital of the company. It is also a sum in respect of any capital withdrawn, within the terms of TA 1988 s 74(f).

---

1 FA 1986 s 87(1).
2 FA 1986 s 87(2)–(5)
3 Inland Revenue Company Tax Manual CT 1760.
4 TA 1988 s 74(f).

> The expenditure is also likely to be disallowable by virtue of TA 1988 s 74(a), because it is not wholly and exclusively laid out or expended for the purposes of the trade. Even where a redemption etc is made "wholly or mainly for the purposes of benefiting a trade carried on by the company" within the terms of TA 1988 s 219 (purchase of own shares by unquoted trading company), it does not follow that the related legal costs are wholly and exclusively for the purposes of the trade.' [1]

To summarise, the Revenue are saying:

1 'on general principles' they are part of the cost of 'changing the share capital'. This is not easy to grasp because of the sloppy wording used. The only way that the share capital is being changed is by the cancellation of the purchased shares. The use of the words 'on general principles' suggests that some asset or advantage of an enduring benefit is being obtained, as suggested by Lord Cave in *British Insulated and Helsby Cables Ltd v Atherton*,[2] or perhaps that some onerous capital asset had been eliminated as in *Mallett v Staveley Coal & Iron Co Ltd*.[3] If so, what is that asset or advantage and is it 'a thing which endures in the way that fixed capital endures'?[4]

2 the expenses are in respect of 'any capital withdrawn'. As there is no definition of 'capital' for this purpose, it should then be given its normal meaning. In the case of a purchase out of distributable profits this is, by definition, not out of capital, at least as far as company law is concerned, so does this argument stand up?

3 the final, and perhaps most persuasive argument is basically that 'wholly and exclusively' is a more rigid requirement than 'wholly or mainly'. In other words, the existence of other, minor, purposes will not prejudice capital treatment for a purchase, but will prevent a deduction for corporation tax purposes.

5.13 It does however seem theoretically possible that a purchase could be effected wholly and exclusively for the purposes of the trade. If a payment to encourage a director to retire can be an allowable expense, as in *Mitchell v B W Noble Ltd*,[5] why then should not a similar payment to encourage a shareholder to depart be allowable? In that case a director of an insurance broker was thought to be guilty of 'misconduct' and under the terms of an earlier agreement he could have been dismissed and required to transfer his shares to the remaining directors at par. However the company feared for its good name (this being 1921) and wanted to avoid any scandal. An agreement was therefore reached whereby the director resigned and received a payment of £19,200. He also agreed to transfer his shares at par, £300, to the remaining directors. These shares were worth considerably more than par having previously attracted a 667% dividend. The existence of the share transfer did not affect the final outcome, as that was merely carrying out the provisions of the earlier agreement which would have applied if the director had been dismissed.

---

1 *Inland Revenue Tax Bulletin*, November 1991.
2 (1926) 10 TC 155.
3 (1928) 13 TC 772.
4 Per Rowlatt J in *Anglo-Persian Oil Co Ltd v Dale* (1931) 16 TC at p 262.
5 (1927) 11 TC 372.

Rowlatt J saw the payment of £19,200 as simply one to get rid of a servant in the course of business and as such could not be said to be a capital payment.[1]

5.14 The main difficulty in trying to justify a deduction for the costs is that a shareholder who is not also involved in the management of the company's business is most unlikely to be disadvantageous to the trade. Therefore to stand any chance of using the decision in *B W Noble*, the vendor would also have to be a director or executive of the company. Such a situation also raises the question of 'golden handshakes' which are discussed in Chapter Ten. The Revenue might seek to distinguish the case from one involving just the purchase of shares by saying they are two quite different transactions. One is to compensate for a breach of contract and the other is to acquire assets, the company's own shares. But of course, as we have already seen, the Revenue accept that the company does not acquire the shares it purchases. What is really happening is that the shareholder is surrendering his or her rights under the company's articles, just as the director is surrendering his or her rights under the service contract.

5.15 However, at the end of the day, it will probably be that the deduction of the expenses is of little consequence when compared to the benefit of the purchase as a whole. There will be little point in even considering a claim unless, quite exceptionally, the presence of the dissenter is causing real problems for the trade. In view of the arguments available to the Revenue, professional advisers should think carefully about the work which they undertake in connection with a purchase of own shares, and in particular who they are advising.

5.16 Consider the question of fees charged for advice in the period leading up to the decision to proceed with a purchase. The situation may be that there is friction between the shareholders which is having a detrimental effect upon the management of the company and thereby its trading performance. A number of possible courses of action may be considered to try and resolve the position. These may include some kind of restructuring of management responsibilities within the company, or a demerger which would attract exempt distribution status.[2] The question of a purchase of own shares to remove a dissident shareholder may be the last resort. The point is that this advice will have been sought in an effort to find a solution to a particular situation which was prejudicial to the trading activities of the company. The advice was not sought to enable the shares to be purchased; that was merely the effect of the advice, not its purpose. Therefore the expense incurred in obtaining that advice was, arguably, incurred wholly and exclusively for the purposes of its trade.

5.17 Even in the case where a founder shareholder is reaching retirement age, the company will need advice on the future management and the structure of the company's business organisation. There may also be decisions to be taken about the funding of the company's future trading operations. The proposed purchase of the founder's shares may be just one proposal coming out of that advice.

1 (1927) 11 TC at p 415.
2 TA 1988 s 213.

The vendor's position

5.18 The reasons for the purchase will dictate whether the vendor may need to be separately advised. If it is a case of the removal of a dissenting shareholder, then a conflict of interest would probably arise for the company's tax adviser and the best course may be to advise the shareholder to seek independent advice. If that is the case, strictly speaking the vendor should bear the cost of that advice. Whether those costs may be deducible in the capital gains computation will in turn depend upon whether they fall within the strict criteria of 'the incidental costs to the vendor of making the disposal'.[1] In the case of a disposal of shares, those costs are restricted to expenditure wholly and exclusively incurred for the purposes of the disposal, being:

1 fees paid for the professional services of any surveyor or valuer, . . . or accountant, or agent or legal adviser;
2 costs of transfer or conveyance;
3 costs reasonably incurred in making any valuation or apportionment required for the purposes of the computation of the gain; and
4 in particular, expenses reasonably incurred in ascertaining market value where required by the capital gains legislation.

5.19 However, in the majority of cases the entire cost will be borne by the company as purchaser, which is customary in company take-over situations. In such a case, is there a tax implication if the shareholder has been separately advised and the company settles the fees for that advice? In theory, if a close company has incurred expense in defraying the liability of a shareholder, that expense would be treated as a distribution.[2] However, that rule is subject to any exceptions provided for in the general distribution rules.[3] It is therefore arguable that the vendor is providing 'new' consideration to the company for the distribution, in the form of his or her agreement to sell the shares. (In a take-over situation however, that rule would not apply as the company incurring the expense would not be doing so for the benefit of its own shareholder; nor would it apply if the acquiring company was a non-close company.)

5.20 Where the vending shareholder is not separately advised, is there a distribution, or perhaps even a benefit in the case of a shareholder/director, where the company settles all the costs of the purchase? Arguably no. Once the actual decision has been taken to purchase the shares, all the steps required by company law and tax law impose obligations upon the company, not on the vendor. It is the company which must:

1 ensure that it has the power to purchase the shares;
2 pass the appropriate special resolution;
3 produce the directors' statutory declaration and auditor's report, if necessary;
4 determine whether the payment is a distribution or not; and
5 apply for any advance clearance from the Revenue.

---

1 TCGA 1992 s38(1)(c).
2 TA 1988 s 418.
3 TA 1988 s 209.

All the vendor has to do is agree the price, hand over the share certificates and, of course, make the appropriate entries on the next tax return.

INTEREST

5.21 Whether a company has or has not retained profits out of which to make the payment for the shares, it will need cash in order to make a valid purchase because it must pay for the shares in full on completion.[1] It may be that the company has to arrange additional borrowings and the question then raised is whether it is entitled to relief for the interest paid on those borrowings.

5.22 Under the new scheme for interest relief for corporation tax purposes introduced in 1996,[2] relief is available for all interest paid by a company. The method of relief, however, will depend upon whether or not its 'loan relationship' is 'for the purposes of a trade'. If that loan is for the purposes of a trade then relief is given as a trading expense. Whilst it may be thought that any loan raised for a purchase of own shares should fall into that category if the purchase qualifies for capital treatment, it is stated that a loan will only be regarded as being for the purposes of a trade if that loan arises 'in the course of activities forming an integral part of that trade'.[3] It is hard to see that purchasing its own shares is an integral part of a company's trade. Therefore the loan gives rise to what is termed a 'non-trading deficit'[4] which, on a claim being made, can be:

1 relieved against total profits of the accounting period;
2 surrendered as group relief;
3 carried back against profits of earlier accounting periods for up to three years, but not against profits for any period before 31 March 1996;[5] or
4 carried forward to set against non-trading profits of subsequent accounting periods.

Any amount not claimed in one of these ways is treated as a non-trading deficit for the next succeeding accounting period.

VALUE ADDED TAX

5.23 There are two points which need to be considered under this heading:

1 whether professional advisers should be charging VAT on their fees; and, if so;
2 whether the company can recover any of that VAT.

---

1 See para 2.5.
2 FA 1996 Part IV Chapter II.
3 FA 1996 s103(2).
4 FA 1996 s 83.
5 FA 1996 Sch 8 para 3(7).

The adviser

5.24 The question is whether the services supplied are standard rated or fall within the exemptions relating to finance.[1] Item 6 of these exemptions covers the 'issue, transfer or receipt of, or any dealing with' any security including shares, whilst item 7 covers 'the making of arrangements for . . . any transaction within item 6'. In addition we are told that item 7 includes 'the introduction to a person effecting transactions in securities . . . within item 6 of a person seeking to acquire or dispose of such securities'.[2]

5.25 It is clear that in the case of a purchase or redemption of own shares, the company itself is not making any supply. As it is paying the consideration for the shares, it is actually receiving the supply. In that case as there would be no transaction within item 6, then item 7 cannot apply and the adviser's fees should be standard rated.

5.26 However, where the purchase or redemption is being financed by a new issue of shares, this issue will be an exempt supply within item 6. Where does this place the adviser? If he or she has prepared all the necessary documentation for the share issue, has he or she 'made arrangements' for that transaction? The legislation and commentary on that legislation has focused upon the corporate finance activities of the merchant banks and large accounting firms. It is not therefore easy to apply the same tests in the context of a transaction envisaged by this work. However, whilst at first sight an adviser might, on a normal interpretation of the term, be regarded as making arrangements, it would seem that Customs use a more restricted definition.

5.27 In a consultation paper issued in November 1994 on the subject of corporate finance Customs said:

> 'Normally professional advisers, such as accountants and solicitors, do not participate in the negotiation of a share transaction and, as such, their services do not come within the scope of the exemption under item [7]'

The dividing line seems to be participation in the negotiations, presumably on price.

5.28 The result of the consultation process was a revision of Customs' leaflet entitled 'Securities'[3] which is still framed in terms of corporate finance and contains the following passage under the heading 'What constitutes making of arrangements'? (sic)

> 'Exemption applies only to the services provided by the party, or possibly the parties (if more than one person is engaged to act as co-ordinator) who actually co-ordinate all of the components of the transaction and conclude it.
>
> This means that exemption only applies to services which are central to the co-ordination of the transaction or its negotiation, including:

1 VATA 1994 Sch 9 Group 5.
2 VATA 1994 Sch 9 Group 5 Note 5.
3 Leaflet 701/44/94.

(i) bringing together sellers/issuers and purchasers/investors;
(ii) carrying out/co-ordinating the necessary negotiations essential to the conclusion of the whole deal;
(iii) instructing/organising and co-ordinating the work of "other" parties involved, eg lawyers, accountants, etc;
(iv) carrying out the necessary consultations with appropriate regulatory bodies;
(v) acting as the central point of contact and execution between the party intending to effect a transaction in securities and their other advisers.

Other parties providing specialist services, eg reporting accountants, legal advisers, document printers are supporting the activities listed above, but their services do not amount to the negotiation or co-ordination of the deal. Such services cannot be regarded as "making arrangements" and therefore are taxable'.

5.29 Again there is reliance on such factors as finding and introducing the parties to the transaction and being involved in negotiating the price. In the case of a purchase or redemption of own shares these features are lacking even if there is also to be an issue of new shares. There is no need to find the parties and very little need, normally, for negotiating. There is therefore no need for anyone to act in the kind of role envisaged by Customs and thus all fees should be standard rated.

5.30 However, in exceptional cases where the adviser is placed in such a role, he or she should analyse the services provided into preparatory advice which would be standard rated and the 'making of arrangements' which would be exempt.

The company

5.31 Input tax can only be recovered 'in so far as the goods and services are used for the purposes of his taxable transactions'[1] and if the goods and services are 'used or to be used for the purpose of any business carried on or to be carried on by him'.[2] Is there therefore a supply to be made by the company to which the receipt of the adviser's services relates?

5.32 As indicated above, if all that is occurring is a purchase or redemption of shares, the company itself is not making any supply. Therefore the input tax could not be directly attributable to the making of an exempt supply. Provided the company only makes taxable supplies, the input tax would be deductible by the company.

5.33 In the case of a company which is affected by the partial exemption provisions[3] the input tax would be residual input tax and would be allowable up to the proportion calculated by comparing taxable supplies to total supplies.[4]

1 EC Sixth Directive (77/388/EEC) Art 17(2).
2 VATA 1994 s 24(1).
3 VATA 1994 s 25; Value Added Tax Regulations 1995 SI 1995/2518 regs 99–111.
4 Value Added Tax Regulations 1995 SI 1995/2518 reg 101(2)(d).

5.34 If the purchase or redemption is to be financed by a new issue of shares, then the company will have made a supply of the issue of shares which falls within the exemption of item 6 of Group 5. It will be important in such a case for the advisers to quantify separately their fees between the share issue and other advice (even if both were standard rated) as the input tax on the former would be directly attributable to an exempt supply by the company and not recoverable, except perhaps under the de minimis rules.[1]

5.35 These rules provide that the exempt input tax can be treated as attributable to taxable supplies if it does not exceed £625 per month on average and does not exceed more than one half of the total input tax for the period concerned. The effect is that for a company which normally only makes taxable supplies, it may still recover VAT of up to £1,875 on fees relating to a share issue for the quarter in which the supply occurs. This is equivalent to fees of £10,714. This input tax recovery will be subject to an annual adjustment[2] and, depending upon the VAT quarter concerned, may result in VAT of up to £7,500 being recoverable for the full VAT year.

1 Value Added Tax Regulations 1995 SI 1995/2518 reg 106.
2 Value Added Tax Regulations 1995 SI 1995/2518 reg 107.

Chapter Six

Is Capital Treatment Really Required?

INDIVIDUALS

6.1 When it first became possible for a company to purchase its own shares there was a significant advantage to the vendor in being granted capital treatment. Capital gains tax for individuals was a maximum 30%, whilst the highest rate of income tax payable on distributions was 75%.

6.2 The abolition of the 15% investment income surcharge in 1984/5 was followed in 1989 by the abolition of the flat rate of capital gains tax and its replacement by the marginal income tax rate which has been a maximum 40% since 1988/89. This has given rise to a position where a prospective vendor needs to consider whether capital treatment will be beneficial or not and how to arrange matters so that the purchase will attract the tax treatment desired. Although the highest rate of tax chargeable is the same under both treatments, it is the method of calculation of the taxable amount and any reliefs available, that will give one treatment an advantage over the other.

6.3 Where a vendor has a relatively high original cost, or 31 March 1982 value as appropriate, the capital treatment will tend to be more favourable. Those who acquired their shares at par after 31 March 1982 will, in the absence of any specific reliefs, be in a position where distribution treatment is preferable even if the capital gains annual exemption is available, unless, exceptionally, the proceeds are less than the annual exemption. In other cases comparative calculations should be prepared to indicate the preferred treatment.

6.4 A further factor introduced into the equation from March 1993 has been the availability of reinvestment relief[1] which offers an opportunity to defer any capital gains tax liability arising from the capital treatment. This obviously would not be available if the purchase were to be regarded as a distribution. Such an opportunity would only really be viable in the case of a dissident shareholder/director looking to invest in another business. It is therefore necessary to ask the prospective vendor what plans he or she has for the proceeds.

6.5 Probably the major factor influencing a need to bring the purchase within the scope of capital treatment is the availability of capital gains tax

---

1 TCGA 1992 s 164A.

retirement relief,[1] especially since the reduction of the qualifying age to 50. However not everyone over that age will be entitled to the full amount of the relief and at the outset a prospective vendor's entitlement should be ascertained. There is little point in aiming for capital treatment if it turns out that the individual is not entitled to retirement relief after all.

6.6 Even without retirement relief it is likely that capital treatment is to be preferred for the majority of individuals. However it is possible to imagine situations where treatment as a distribution would be advantageous:

1 where a shareholder who was also a sole trader or partner had unrelieved trading losses available for the year which might otherwise be unused. Whilst these losses would eliminate any higher rate tax due on the distribution, they would not result in any repayment of tax credits;[2] (prior to 5 December 1996 the tax credits attaching to a distribution could be repaid); and
2 where the individual's cost of acquisition, or 31 March 1982 value if appropriate, is less than the nominal value of the shares being purchased by the company, so that the amount of the distribution was less than the amount of the chargeable gain.

TRUSTS

Interest in possession trusts

6.7 These are trusts where one or more beneficiaries are entitled to the trust income as it arises but have no entitlement to the trust capital except by virtue of the exercise of the trustees' discretion or some future contingency specified under the terms of the trust. Such trusts are also commonly called 'life interest' trusts and the beneficiaries 'life tenants' (or, in Scotland, life renters) even though their entitlement to income may be by reference to periods other than their own lifetime.

The trustees' position

6.8 Trustees of interest in possession trusts are liable to both capital gains tax and income tax at the basic rate. If the purchase is treated as a distribution, the trustees are deemed to receive income which has suffered lower rate income tax which is sufficient to satisfy their income tax liability but which is not repayable.[3] Normally these trusts do not pay tax at the rate applicable to trusts on income[4] because the income arising under the trust is not to be accumulated nor is it payable at the trustees' discretion. However, with effect from 5 December 1996, a charge to tax at the trust rate has been imposed where a purchase of own shares occurs from trustees which is treated as a distribution.[5]

---

1 TCGA 1992 s 163.
2 FA 1997 Sch 7 para 2(1) and TA 1988 s 246D(2)(b).
3 TA 1988 s 246D(4).
4 Under TA 1988 s 686.
5 FA 1997 Sch 7 para 3.

The beneficiary's position

6.9 The measure of the life tenant's income from the trust is the share of the trustees' net statutory income to which he or she is entitled. Whilst a distribution clearly forms part of the trustees' statutory income, it is not something to which the life tenant is entitled. Under trust law the proceeds of the share sale are part of the trust capital and, by definition, someone who has an interest in possession is not interested in the trust capital.

6.10 Readers looking for some comfort for this last statement may be interested in comments extracted from the Revenue's consultative document on trusts published in 1991.[1] After discussing the treatment of interest in possession trusts with regard to 'deemed' income charges under the accrued income scheme, offshore income gains and deep discount gains, it went on to say:[2]

> 'Such deemed income largely arises from transactions involving trust capital and does not affect the tax position of the beneficiaries. It is proposed that deemed income should remain, as at present, taxable only in the hands of the trustees. As the interest in possession beneficiaries will not generally be entitled to receive the underlying profits, it would not be appropriate to deem those profits to be their income for tax purposes.'

Later[3] it said:

> 'Deemed income is not treated as the interest in possession beneficiary's income for tax purposes, as the corresponding capital receipt generally does not belong to that beneficiary.'

Discretionary / accumulation and maintenance trusts

6.11 These are trusts where no beneficiary has any current entitlement to income or capital of the trust except when the trustees exercise their discretion in his or her favour.

The trustees' position

6.12 Trustees of these settlements are liable to tax at 34% on capital gains and income arising to them which is either to be accumulated or is payable at their discretion.[4] The proceeds of a share sale are, as stated, capital. They are not, therefore, income arising to the trustees, nor are they income which is required to be accumulated or is payable at the discretion of the trustees and consequently would normally be outside the scope of income tax. However, in common with interest in possession trusts, a charge to tax at the trust rate has been imposed with effect from 5 December 1996 on any purchase or redemption which is treated as a distribution.

The beneficiary's position

6.13 A charge at 34% is imposed on payments made by trustees in the exercise of their discretion which, for the purposes of the Income Tax Acts are

1 '*The Income Tax and Capital Gains Tax Treatment of Resident Trusts*'.
2 At para 5.15.
3 At para 7.4.
4 TA 1988 s 686(2).

income in the hands of the recipient.[1] Credit is given for the 'pool' of tax paid on income as it has arisen.[2] However, even if the proceeds of the share sale were to be distributed to the beneficiaries by virtue of the exercise of the trustees' discretion, it is arguable that such payments are not income in the hands of the recipients. In the leading case on this point[3] it was held that a payment out of trust capital in the exercise of a power over capital could not create an income interest even if that payment were made in a number of instalments. It should however be remembered that a payment of capital out of a discretionary trust may give rise to an exit charge for inheritance tax purposes.[4]

Income tax void trusts

6.14 However, where a trust is ineffective for income tax purposes[5] because the settlor retains an interest in the settlement, usually because he or his spouse is a beneficiary, the settlor will be chargeable at 40% on the total of the distribution received by the trustees plus the attached tax credit. This is because, although the proceeds constitute a capital receipt under trust law, they are a distribution[6] and because they are therefore 'chargeable to income tax by deduction or otherwise'[7] they are within the definition of 'income arising under a settlement' and can be assessed on the settlor.[8] In such a situation the settlor has a statutory right to recover the tax he has paid from the trustees.[9]

Conclusion

6.15 Where trustees are concerned, whether distribution or capital treatment is preferable will be a case of making a comparison of the tax rates applicable and the amount of 'profit' which is assessable.

Example

The Moriarty Trust sells 10,000 £1 shares in Greenslade Ltd back to the company for £100,000.

If the shares were acquired at par in 1987, the tax liability would be based upon the 'profit' of £90,000 (ignoring for these purposes indexation relief). If distribution treatment applied, the tax liability would be calculated as follows:

---

1 TA 1988 s 687(1).
2 TA 1988 s 687(3).
3 *Stevenson v Wishart* [1987] STC 266.
4 IHTA 1984 s 65.
5 ie it falls within TA 1988 Part XV.
6 TA 1988 s 209.
7 TA 1988 s 660G(3).
8 TA 1988 s 660A.
9 TA 1988 s 660D.

Distribution	90,000
Tax credit	22,500
	112,500
Tax at 34%	38,250
less tax credit	22,500
Tax due	15,750

or expressed another way, 17.5% of the 'profit'.
If capital treatment applied, the trustees would pay capital gains tax at 23% on the 'profit', subject to the annual exemption, if it were an interest in possession trust and 34% otherwise.

However, if the shares had been purchased by the trustees for £70,000, then although the tax under the distribution treatment would remain at £15,750, the tax under the capital treatment on the gain of £30,000 would be £6,900 if an interest in possession trust or £10,200 otherwise (ignoring any annual exemptions).

PERSONAL REPRESENTATIVES

6.16 A personal representative of a deceased shareholder is deemed to have acquired the shares at the market value at the date of death of that shareholder. As a purchase of own shares from a personal representative is likely to be at the market value prevailing at that time, it may well be that there is little difference between the value at the date of death and at the date of purchase. Therefore capital treatment will obviously be preferred.

6.17 Personal representatives may have both possible routes to capital treatment open to them. They may be able to claim that the sale is for the benefit of the trade in that they wish to realise the value of the shareholding and would otherwise be unwilling shareholders.[1] Alternatively they may claim that the sale is necessary in order to raise funds to pay inheritance tax on the deceased's estate. In that case they would have to show that undue hardship would otherwise result.[2]

6.18 When it comes to qualifying for capital treatment under the trading benefit route, personal representatives are in a slightly better position than other vendors. They will satisfy the ownership test where the deceased held the shares for only three years instead of the usual five. It is a curious fact that there could therefore be cases where a shareholder's death would be quite fortuitous in enabling the ownership test to be satisfied where it would not have been if he had lived. It is doubtful whether this particular loophole has really been exploited voluntarily.

6.19 Where it is desired that the company should purchase the shares of a deceased shareholder and there has been a considerable increase in value since death, consideration might be given to whether these shares could be

1 See para 2 of SP 2/82.
2 TA 1988 s 219(2).

sold by the personal representatives whilst the estate is being administered. Alternatively, they could distribute the shares to the legatee who would then sell them to the company. The attraction of a sale by the personal representatives is that they will only pay capital gains tax at 23% should any gain arise, whereas the legatee could face a 40% liability. The choice of method will depend upon the nature of the legatee's interest.

6.20 If the legatee is entitled to the shares as a specific legacy, the personal representatives will be prevented from selling the shares.[1] The order in which personal representatives may have recourse to the assets in the estate in order to meet the payment of the deceased's liabilities and the administrative expenses is strictly prescribed. In simple terms they would have recourse to the assets comprised in the residue and, only after those had been exhausted, would they be able to sell assets which had been the subject of specific legacies.

6.21 Where, however, the shares form part of the residue, the personal representatives will be able to choose between those shares and other assets when raising funds to meet liabilities and their lower capital gains rate may be a factor in that decision. On the other hand it should be remembered that if full business property relief were not available for any reason and inheritance tax arises on the value of the shares themselves, the sale of the shares would have the effect of withdrawing the benefit of any instalment relief for payment of that tax.

LEGATEES

6.22 For the same reasons as mentioned under the heading for personal representatives, a legatee will normally have a base cost which is not significantly below the purchase proceeds.

6.23 In this context it should be remembered that although the shares may not have been transferred to the legatee until the estate has been fully administered, he is deemed to have acquired them at the date of the deceased's death.[2] In the majority of cases, therefore, capital treatment will be preferred.

6.24 In common with personal representatives, the ownership test is reduced to three years and credit is given for the length of ownership by the deceased.

6.25 A legatee may also be entitled to capital treatment on the grounds of having to meet an inheritance tax liability where he is liable for that tax on a specific legacy which bears its own tax or, it is suggested, in respect of an earlier potentially exempt transfer which became chargeable as a result of the death of the deceased. Indeed, on a close reading of the legislation it appears that the inheritance tax may arise as a result of the death of someone other than a deceased shareholder.[3]

---

1 By Administration of Estates Act 1925 First Schedule.
2 TA 1988 s 62(4).
3 See however para 4.43.

CORPORATE VENDORS

6.26 In the early years following the introduction of legislation permitting the purchase of own shares it was felt that distribution treatment was preferable for corporate vendors because dividends from UK resident companies are franked investment income and therefore exempt from corporation tax.[1]

6.27 In one of the shortest and clearest sections in the Taxes Acts, it states:

> 'Except as otherwise provided by the Corporation Tax Acts, corporation tax shall not be chargeable on dividends and other distributions of a company resident in the United Kingdom, nor shall any such dividends or distributions be taken into account in computing income for corporation tax.'

6.28 In addition it was felt that because amounts chargeable to income tax are excluded from the consideration chargeable to capital gains tax,[2] a significant capital loss could arise where the shares had a base cost in excess of the nominal value.

6.29 Whilst the Revenue accept that the distribution itself is exempt from corporation tax, they issued the following Statement of Practice in April 1989[3] which set out a revised view that, in the resulting capital gains tax computation, the distribution element did not fall to be excluded from the taxable consideration.

> 'If the purchase of its own shares by a company resident in the UK gives rise to a distribution, and a shareholder receiving such a distribution is itself a company, the distribution is included in the consideration for the disposal of the shares for the purposes of the charge to corporation tax on chargeable gains. In the Revenue's view the effect of TA 1988 ss 208, 345(3) [now TCGA 1992 s 37(1)] is that the distribution does not suffer a tax charge as income within the terms of [TCGA 1992 s 37(1)]. The Revenue will apply this Statement of Practice where a company purchases its own shares after 19 April 1989.'

6.30 The Revenue's view is that consideration is only excluded from the capital gains computation where it has been charged to income tax as income of the person making the disposal for the purposes of the Income Tax Acts. Although it is provided that any reference to income tax and the Income Tax Acts shall, in relation to a company, be construed as references to corporation tax and the Corporation Tax Acts,[4] the distribution element is removed from the scope of corporation tax because distributions from UK companies are exempt from corporation tax.[5] Therefore no deduction should be made from the consideration in computing the chargeable gain or allowable loss on the disposal.

6.31 That argument does have a certain logic to it. However, it overlooks the fact that companies do not pay capital gains tax; they pay corporation tax on

1 TA 1988 s 208.
2 TCGA 1992 s 37.
3 Statement of Practice SP 4/89.
4 TCGA 1992 s 8(4).
5 TA 1988 s 208.

both income and chargeable gains. According to the Revenue's view the distribution element of the proceeds will be chargeable to corporation tax on chargeable gains. But, as we have seen, it is specifically stated that the distribution is not liable to corporation tax! This position is most unsatisfactory and it is perhaps surprising that no challenge to the Revenue's view has been mounted. The legislation in this area clearly fails to cater sensibly for corporate vendors.

6.32 On this point, a forceful argument is made by Richard Bramwell QC and his fellow authors[1] that dividends received by a UK resident company from another such company may give rise to chargeable gains. The argument may be summarised as follows:

1 where a 'capital distribution' is received in respect of a holding of shares, there is deemed to be a disposal of an interest in those shares;[2]
2 a 'capital distribution' means 'any distribution from a company...in money or money's worth, except a distribution which in the hands of the recipient constitutes income for the purposes of corporation tax';[3] and
3 as dividends are not part of a company's income for corporation tax purposes, they must be 'capital distributions'.[4]

6.33 An alternative argument is:

1 if a sum is excluded from the capital gains computation on the grounds that it is chargeable to corporation tax as income, it is not a 'capital sum';[5]
2 conversely, therefore, following the Revenue's line of argument, if a dividend from a UK company or other distribution is not to be excluded from the capital gains computation because it is not within the charge to corporation tax, it must be a capital sum; and
3 the receipt of a 'capital sum' is treated as a disposal notwithstanding that no asset is acquired by the payer of the sum.[6] Therefore receipt of a dividend will give rise to a disposal.

6.34 These arguments were put to the Revenue and their response, whilst interesting, is unsatisfactory:

> 'SP4/89 is concerned with the case where there is an actual disposal of shares within the ordinary meaning of the term. Such a case is governed by section 37(1) TCGA rather than section 122 TCGA, which deems there to be a disposal for capital gains purposes on receipt of a capital distribution in respect of shares.
>
> The terms of SP4/89 in relation to company purchases of own shares are not regarded as affecting the established Revenue view that franked investment income and group income are not capital distributions within section

1 *Taxation of Companies and Company Reconstructions* 6th Edition paras 13–23.
2 TCGA 1992 s 122(1).
3 TCGA 1992 s 122(5)(b) as amended by TCGA 1992 s 8(4) for corporation tax purposes.
4 TA 1988 s 208.
5 TCGA 1992 s 22(3).
6 TCGA 1992 s 22(1).

122(5)(b). This provision employs a different test from that in section 37(1) referred to in the Statement of Practice.

Distributions which are not capital distributions for the purposes of section 122 establish an exception to which the rule in section 22 is subject, Franked Investment Income or group income excluded from the definition of 'capital distribution' in section 122(5)(b) would not therefore be treated by section 22 as consideration for a capital gains disposal.

The suggestion that there is a possible argument that all distributions received by one UK resident company from another are consideration received on a part disposal for capital gains purposes is inconsistent with the frame of reference pre-supposed by section 177 TCGA and section 30 TCGA.'

6.35 In this response the Revenue seem to be trying to draw a distinction between dividends and other distributions. Bramwell is not persuaded that such a distinction is permissible because of the wording of paragraph 1 of Schedule F, especially '. . . all such distributions shall be regarded as income however they fall to be dealt with in the hands of the recipient.'

6.36 During 1991, as a result of correspondence with the Technical Committee of the Chartered Institute of Taxation, the Revenue wrote to expand upon the position set out in SP 4/89. The following note was published:[1]

'In April 1989 the Inland Revenue issued a Statement of Practice (SP 4/89) notifying a change of practice in the capital gains treatment of a distribution received by a corporate shareholder as a result of a company's purchase of its own shares. The Revenue's view was that sections 208 [ICTA 1988] and [s 8(4) TCGA 1992] precluded the exclusion of the distribution from the consideration for the disposal of the shares for the purposes of the charge to corporation tax on chargeable gains. Previously, section [37(1) TCGA 1992] had been considered to permit the deduction of the distribution from the consideration.

The Revenue have now confirmed in correspondence that the change in practice outlined in SP 4/89 does not extend to a redemption of shares held by a corporate shareholder. An extract from their letter appears below:

"Statement of Practice SP 4/89 sets out the Revenue's view of the capital gains treatment where a company resident in the UK purchases its own shares and a distribution is received by a corporate shareholder. The Statement of Practice deals only with company own share purchases, and I can confirm that the Revenue accepts different considerations apply to a redemption of redeemable shares. In the Revenue's view a distribution received by a corporate shareholder on a redemption of shares by a UK resident company falls within section [122 TCGA 1992] rather than section [37(1) TCGA 1992]. In such cases the distribution is accordingly not part of the consideration for capital gains purposes.

There is no present intention to issue a further Statement of Practice dealing with the capital gains treatment of share redemptions. Concerning your request for an explanation of the Revenue's analysis of these issues, it is of course open to a company, in relation to its

1 *Taxation Practitioner* December 1991, p 545.

> own tax liabilities, to contend for a result different from that set out in SP 4/89. In these circumstances, detailed discussion of the underlying issues is I think more properly a matter to be addressed in a particular case rather than in general correspondence.
>
> The comments in this letter set out the Revenue's understanding of the law at the present time. The tax treatment of any particular transaction would of course fall to be dealt with by reference to the law and practice then prevailing."

The point appears to be that a redemption of shares in accordance with the rights in the company's articles of association is regarded by the Revenue as a capital distribution to the extent that the amount received does not constitute income for the purposes of income tax or corporation tax [s 122(5)]. Section [122(1)] tells us that the shareholder is to 'be treated as if he had in consideration of that capital distribution disposed of an interest in the shares'. Thus, the distribution part of the redemption amount never falls to be included in the consideration for the deemed disposal which occurs on redemption because the Revenue apparently regard it as constituting income in the hands of the recipient, notwithstanding their controversial view of the status of distributions in the context of section 208 ICTA 1988.'

6.37 As reported at the end of that note, the Revenue seemed to be saying that a redemption rather than a purchase of shares would attract a more favourable treatment. This view seems less justifiable than that expressed in SP 4/89 and seems to proceed along the following lines:

1 the redemption constitutes a 'capital distribution',[1] which is defined as any distribution except one which in the hands of the recipient constitutes income for the purposes of income tax (or corporation tax);
2 because it is a capital distribution, it cannot be taxable as income and thereby cannot be excluded from the capital gains consideration;[2] but
3 the distribution is not part of the consideration for capital gains purposes.

6.38 With all due respect to whoever composed the response on behalf of the Revenue, this argument does not add up and stems from the basic viewpoint that there is a fundamental difference between a purchase and a redemption for capital gains purposes. In the Revenue's internal instructions, Inspectors are advised that a repayment or redemption of share capital is not a sale and only becomes a disposal by the operation of s 122.[3] This view is quite unobjectionable where a company is repaying some part of the share capital and the recipients still hold their shares. There is, in that situation, a need to deem a disposal to occur, although it would seem that the situation is already catered for by the rule that says a disposal occurs when a capital sum is derived from an asset.[4]

6.39 In the case of a redemption, whilst there is no acquisition by the company, the shareholder has clearly disposed of his rights. They have gone, they are no more, there has, by definition, been an actual disposal, so why should

1 Within TCGA 1992 s 122.
2 By virtue of TCGA 1992 s 37.
3 Inland Revenue Capital Gains Manual CG 58655
4 TCGA 1992 s 22.

s 122 be in point? That section applies where a capital distribution is received by a shareholder who retains ownership of the shares in respect of which the distribution is made. It serves to create a deemed disposal where no actual disposal would otherwise have occurred.

6.40 During the preparation of this work, the Revenue were approached under the Open Government Initiative and asked three questions:

1 whether the comments on SP4/89 at paragraph **6.29** were an acceptable summary of their views;
2 whether the comments on their letter to the Technical Committee of The Chartered Institute of Taxation at paragraph **6.36** were also an acceptable summary of their views; and
3 could they justify the comments they made in 1991 in the light of the points made above about s 122?

Unfortunately on this occasion Government was not 'Open' nor was anyone showing any 'Initiative'. It was claimed that 'The resources required to consider the various references you mention and their interpretation in the context of your letter would be extensive and would require unreasonable diversion of resources.' It therefore seems that either the Revenue's policy in this area is so obscure that it cannot be easily explained, or that it does not wish to admit that the policy cannot be justified.

6.41 Until such time as the Revenue's views have been clarified or successfully challenged, it is obviously prudent to plan on the basis of known Revenue practice, the effect of which will be that there will be no difference between capital and distribution treatment where the corporate vendor acquired the shares at par. It would also seem prudent for companies taking minority stakes in other companies to do so by means of redeemable rather then irredeemable shares.

CHARITIES, PENSION FUNDS AND OTHER TAX-EXEMPT PERSONS

6.42 In cases where the vendor is not liable to income tax or capital gains tax, it might be assumed at first sight that there was no particular advantage in either capital or distribution treatment. However, with distribution treatment, the fact that the vendor could claim a repayment of the tax credit associated with the distribution meant that the company could take that opportunity of reducing the purchase price of the shares. These are the circumstances behind the case of *IRC v Universities Superannuation Scheme Ltd.*[1]

6.43 Universities Superannuation Scheme Ltd (USS) was the trustee of an exempt approved pension scheme. In 1984 it invested in a development company, TSH, which was developing a business park near Heathrow Airport.

1 [1997] STC 1.

That investment took the form of a loan of £25 million, at a rate which was accepted to be less than a normal commercial rate, and a subscription for 10,000 A ordinary shares at a premium of £9 per share, making a total cost of £100,000. There was a put option which gave USS the right to require TSH's parent company, 'Stockley', to purchase the A shares for a sum equal to 7.5% of the net asset value of TSH.

6.44 USS were advised to exercise that option in 1988 and would have received a sum of £3,517,000 from Stockley for those shares. However, as a result of subsequent negotiations, USS actually sold the shares back to TSH itself but for only £2,662,750. As the shares had been held for less than five years, capital treatment was not applicable and a distribution of £2,562,750 arose, (being the excess over the repayment of share capital of £100,000). Being an exempt body, USS could reclaim the associated tax credit of £854,250, which fortuitously brought its total receipts upto £3,517,000, the amount it would have received if the shares had been purchased by Stockley as originally intended.

6.45 The Revenue, whilst originally repaying the tax credit, later issued a notice[1] that an assessment was required to be raised to counteract a 'tax advantage' allegedly obtained by USS by the receipt of 'an abnormal amount by way of dividend'.[2] The appeal against that notice subsequently came before the Special Commissioner in February 1995. There were three questions to consider:

1 whether the exemption from tax of a body such as USS was a 'relief from tax' within the definition of a 'tax advantage';
2 whether USS had received an 'abnormal' amount by way of dividend; and
3 whether the transaction was carried out for bona fide commercial reasons or in the ordinary course of making or managing investments.

6.46 The actual decision was a mere formality as, on the first question, the Commissioner was bound by the High Court decision of Aldous J in *Sheppard and another (Trustees of the Woodland Trust) v IRC (No2)*[3] in which it was held that trustees of a tax-exempt body could not obtain a 'tax advantage' within the definition of that phrase.[4] Aldous J quoted from Lord Wilberforce's speech in *IRC v Parker*[5] and then continued:

> 'The whole idea of a tax advantage is that the taxpayer has done something which allows him to resist an assessment and the Revenue can point to something which alters his position to his advantage. To adopt the words of Lord Wilberforce, "there must be a contrast as regards the 'receipts' between the actual case where these accrue in a non-taxable way with a possible accruer in a taxable way, and unless this contrast exists, the existence of the advantage is not established."'

1 Under TA 1988 s 703(3).
2 TA 1988 s 704 Circumstance A.
3 [1993] STC 240.
4 In TA 1988 s 709(1).
5 (1964) 43 TC at p 441.

6.47 There was therefore no need for the Special Commissioner to consider the second and third questions, but as he was invited to pass judgment, he held that the 'dividend'[1] was not 'abnormal' in the light of the investment as a whole, but found for the Revenue by holding that the transaction was not one which was in the ordinary course of making or managing investments.

6.48 The case is of interest in that before the Special Commissioner, no evidence was presented as to the reasons why the terms of the option were suddenly waived. We are led to believe that the solicitor acting for USS 'didn't find out why' the identity of the purchaser was to be changed and this came about from a casual remark made during a car journey. It seems also to have been suggested to the Special Commissioner that the change may have been that TSH had more cash resources than Stockley. Despite all that reticence and apparent uncertainty, the reality, of course, is that the plan was to save Stockley over £854,000 on the deal, whilst ensuring that USS would not be out of pocket because it would receive a corresponding Revenue subsidy. One can only guess that it must have been the decision to disregard the option terms that annoyed the Revenue. Had the original option required TSH to purchase the shares rather than Stockley, then perhaps this case would not have arisen.

6.49 Inevitably, the Revenue appealed to the High Court[2] where Sir John Vinelott declined to follow the decision in *Woodland Trust*, explaining that Lord Wilberforce's remarks in *IRC v Parker* were directed at the words in the final part of the definition of a 'tax advantage' and did not apply to the opening words, 'a relief or increased relief from, or repayment or increased repayment of, tax . . .'. Therefore it was held that an exempt body could obtain a tax advantage. The remaining questions were remitted to the tribunal[3] to determine whether the dividend was abnormal and whether USS fell within the escape clause.

6.50 As a consequence of this case and others the Revenue took steps to limit the damage. It was announced that action was to be taken to prevent the repayment of tax credits where a purchase of own shares ranked as a distribution.[4] Legislation was introduced with effect from 8 October 1996[5] which treats a distribution which takes the form of a purchase or redemption of its own shares as if it were a Foreign Income Dividend. The effect is that, whilst the company still has to account for advance corporation tax, there is no tax credit attaching to that distribution. Individuals or trustees are, however, treated as having received the distribution after the deduction of the lower rate of income tax, but that notional tax is not repayable.[6] As far as pension funds and charities are concerned, the lack of a tax credit means there can be no 'Revenue subsidy' as was sought in the case of USS.

---

1 This term also includes distributions generally.
2 [1997] STC 1.
3 Which has specific jurisdiction in these matters – TA 1988 s 705(2).
4 And also in cases where a 'special dividend' is paid which is in some way referable to a transaction in securities.
5 FA 1997 s 69 and Sch 7.
6 TA 1988 s 246D(1) and (2).

THE PURCHASING COMPANY

6.51 This chapter has so far concentrated on whether different types of vendor would prefer distribution or capital treatment. Looking at the position from the point of view of the purchasing company, it would always prefer the purchase to be accorded capital treatment. This avoids any liability to advance corporation tax. That liability is precisely what it says; a payment of corporation tax in advance. At best it causes a cash flow disadvantage by paying tax earlier than necessary. At worst it is effectively a direct cost. This latter situation arises where the company cannot obtain relief either in the current year or by carrying back[1] due to an insufficiency of profits.

1 TA 1988 s 239(1) and (3).

Chapter Seven

BREAKING THE CONDITIONS FOR CAPITAL TREATMENT

7.1 Having decided that distribution treatment is actually preferable, taxpayers may find themselves in the unfortunate position where they satisfy all the conditions for capital treatment to apply. They therefore need to consider what steps can be taken to avoid a section of the Taxes Acts which was introduced as a relieving provision. A layman may be forgiven for thinking that if a taxpayer did not wish to avail himself of a tax relief it would be a simple matter to elect for that relief not to apply. Unfortunately laymen are not responsible for our tax legislation and hapless taxpayers will have to take steps to avoid capital treatment and need to consider how to fail the various tests.

THE STATUS TEST

7.2 This is perhaps the easiest test to fail, by the simple expedient of transferring the shares to a non-resident/non-ordinarily resident nominee prior to the sale. Having said that, there will be some individuals who may balk at the idea of transferring shares to someone living in a foreign country who they have never met, even if that person is a respectable tax adviser, lawyer or accountant.

7.3 It has been suggested that the Revenue could seek to apply the principle established in *Furniss v Dawson.*[1] The argument is that the transfer into the name of a non-resident nominee is a step inserted into a pre-ordained series of transactions which, of itself, serves no commercial purpose and it should therefore be ignored. It is difficult to find fault with this argument. One can only presume that, in practice, the Revenue adopt the Nelsonian approach to such cases and are normally content to allow taxpayers effectively to elect for distribution treatment in this way. This sanguine attitude may, in part, be due to a realisation that if the *Furniss v Dawson* principle were applied, it would prove that the purchase was part of a scheme or arrangement being carried out for tax avoidance reasons and capital treatment would not be available in any event.[2]

1 [1984] STC 153, 55 TC 324.
2 TA 1988 s 219(1)(a).

THE OWNERSHIP TEST

7.4 Individuals who have already achieved the required five year ownership and are seeking to fail this test, need a mechanism whereby they can divest themselves of the beneficial ownership of the shares. This needs to be done without incurring a capital gains tax liability but at the same time ensuring that the sales proceeds are applied for their own benefit.

7.5 Such a mechanism is an interest in possession settlement whereby the individual settles the shares on trust under which he or she has an interest in possession and the trustees have the power to advance capital for his or her benefit. As the shares will be in a trading company (which they must be because, if they were not, capital treatment would not be available anyway) gift hold-over relief from capital gains tax would be available.[1] The gift would be a non-event for inheritance tax purposes because beneficiaries entitled to interests in possession are deemed to have beneficial ownership of the assets in which their interest subsists. There will be no loss in value to the individual's estate and accordingly no transfer of value. The transfer to the trustees will start a new five-year period and a purchase from them will not satisfy the ownership test. Because the individual is both the settlor and the beneficiary, any trust income, including the distribution on the purchase of the shares, will be assessed on him or her.[2] Again the comments made above about the potential application of the *Furniss v Dawson* principle are relevant here.

7.6 It is not possible to fail this test by transferring the shares to a spouse, because he or she would obtain the benefit of the ownership of the other spouse. Curiously, the Revenue are reported to refuse clearance for capital treatment where there are gifts of shares to a spouse shortly before the purchase by the company. This is on the grounds that this indicates that the purchase was part of a scheme for the avoidance of tax. However it would be unwise to rely upon an inter-spouse gift to achieve distribution treatment.

7.7 The more imaginative may hypothesise a situation where the individual gifts the shares to an adult child who then sells them on to the company. Gift hold-over relief would be due on the gift and the sale by the child would attract distribution treatment. Provided the child kept the proceeds this should achieve its objective. But, if those proceeds were to find their way back to the parent, the Revenue could argue, with some justification, that beneficial ownership of the shares had never passed to the child (and indeed was never intended to pass). That child was merely acting as nominee or bare trustee for the parent. Such a strategy would only be practical if the parent had intended to make gifts to the child out of the sales proceeds.

7.8 In the case of a corporate vendor, it is possible to breach the ownership test by transferring the shares to another member of the same group of companies, or failing that, to a wholly owned subsidiary formed especially for that

---

1 TCGA 1992 s 165.
2 TA 1988 s 660A.

purpose. No chargeable gain would arise on the transfer because of the exemption for intra-group transfers.[1] As there is no provision allowing ownership by the transferor company to be deemed to be that of the transferee, a new period of ownership will commence.

THE TRADING BENEFIT TEST

7.9 Perhaps the easiest, and least contentious method of breaching the trading benefit test would be for the vendor to remain involved in the management of the company on a full-time basis following the purchase. It would be impossible for the Revenue to take exception to this as there are no artificial steps being taken. The individual simply continues as he or she has always done. Clearly this is not a practical possibility in cases where it is sought to remove a dissident shareholder/director.

7.10 In cases where the vendor is not also a director or otherwise engaged in the management of the company's business, there may be cases where it is difficult to see how the trade could be said to benefit from the purchase of the shares, despite the Revenue's apparent acceptance to the contrary.[2] It would therefore be possible to suggest, in a case involving a small minority holding, that the purchase of shares from an unwilling shareholder would not have any beneficial impact on the trade. Obviously, any claims that purchases of shares would not benefit the trade must be made with great care so as not to prejudice any subsequent cases involving the same company where capital treatment may be desired.

7.11 The trading benefit test is considered in more detail in Chapter Eight. Before leaving this topic, however, it is worth remembering that besides benefiting the trade, the purchase must not form part of a scheme or arrangement for the avoidance of tax. So in theory it is quite possible for a taxpayer who is seeking distribution treatment to write to the Revenue and say 'I am going to sell my shares to the company and deliberately breach the conditions for capital treatment for the sole reason of avoiding the increased tax I would have to pay if I satisfied those conditions'. Would the Revenue ever write back and say that they did not accept there was a tax avoidance motive?

7.12 Attractive as this argument is, it is perhaps the tax equivalent of Pandora's Box and should only be used as an absolute last resort. It has been suggested that the Revenue might seek to apply the anti-avoidance legislation relating to the cancellation of tax advantages arising from transactions in securities[3] in such circumstances. This seems an unlikely weapon for the Revenue to choose. After all, the basic thrust of these provisions is to take a capital receipt and deem it to be income, which is precisely what the taxpayer

---

1 TCGA 1992 s 171.
2 See para 8.17.
3 TA 1988 s 703.

was trying to achieve anyway. In order to apply the provisions the Revenue would have to show:

1 that there was a transaction in securities;
2 that a 'tax advantage' had been obtained as a consequence of that transaction; and
3 that the advantage had been obtained in one of five 'prescribed circumstances'.[1]

7.13 There is clearly a transaction in securities, so the next consideration is whether a 'tax advantage' has been obtained. In this context, 'tax' is defined as either income tax or corporation tax.[2] As the intention in the case of a vendor other than a company is to avoid capital gains tax, this anti-avoidance provision cannot apply. This point seems to be accepted by the Revenue.[3]

THE CONNECTION TEST

7.14 This can be a hard test to satisfy, relying as it does on the vendor's associates. Conversely, it is easy to fail. The commonest way of failing this test is for the vendor to leave the sales proceeds outstanding on loan account with the company so that he is then entitled to more than 30% of the company's share and loan capital. A slight complication is that under the Companies Act the proceeds must be paid in full on completion.[4] Therefore it is necessary for the vendor and the company to exchange cheques for identical amounts on completion.

THE SUBSTANTIAL REDUCTION TEST

7.15 This test will not be satisfied if the vendor's shareholding (together with those of his associates) has not fallen by more than 25% of what it was before the purchase. However, the test is only applicable where the individual does not sell the whole of his shareholding. Therefore the tactic would be to sell only part of the shareholding so that the test is applicable and is not satisfied. In a simple case, a sale of shares in tranches could be considered, although there will be a danger that the final tranche may qualify for capital treatment as the test will not then be applicable.

7.16 Where associates are in existence it may be possible, subject to the exact holdings, to arrange matters so that the final tranche is insignificant.

---

1 TA 1988 s 704.
2 TA 1988 s 832(3).
3 Inland Revenue Inspector's Manual IM 4513.
4 CA 1985 s 159(3).

Example

Dennis holds 200 shares in Ellington Ltd out of 1,000 shares in issue. His associates hold a further 400. If he were to sell his entire holding the test would not be applicable and, all other tests being satisfied, he would qualify for capital treatment. On the other hand if he were to sell only 199 shares, his percentage holding (including that of his associates) will have fallen from 60% to 50% (401 out of 801), a reduction of only 16.6%. The substantial reduction test will apply and will not be satisfied.

7.17 It may also be possible to arrange matters so that the holdings of other shareholders are changed and thereby the vendor could be, or would remain, connected.

Example

The shares in Crun's Bank Ltd are held:

Henry	500
Minnie (his wife)	100
Neddie (his adult son)	400
	1,000

Henry founded the company in June 1982 and his base cost for capital gains tax purposes is therefore £500. He is 45 years old. The company has been very successful and now Henry wishes to take out £1m from the company and retire. This amount equates to the open market value of 450 shares. All the conditions for capital treatment would be satisfied and he faces a capital gain of almost £1m and a tax liability of £400,000.

If distribution treatment applied, Henry would be liable to higher rate tax on a distribution of almost £1m plus the associated tax credit of £250,000. After setting off the tax credit his tax liability will be £250,000, a saving over the capital treatment of £160,000.

If Henry sells 450 shares to the company, the substantial reduction test will be satisfied as the combined holdings of Henry and Minnie will fall from 60% to 27.2%, a reduction of 54.6%. The connection test would also be satisfied.

However, if Neddie were to sell 50 shares to the company at the same time as Henry's sale, the resulting holdings would be:

Henry	50
Minnie (his wife)	100
Neddie (his adult son)	350
	500

The combined holding of Henry and Minnie would then be 30% and the connection test would be breached. Neddie, meanwhile, has increased his percentage holding from 40% to 70%.

CONCLUSION

7.18 Until such time as sanity prevails and capital treatment is only available by election (and the satisfaction of the various tests), taxpayers will have to continue to seek ways of avoiding that 'relief'. The appropriate way will depend upon the circumstances in which the purchase is to take place. The company, of course, is more likely to co-operate with a retiring shareholder/director than with a dissident.

Chapter Eight

THE TRADING BENEFIT TEST

8.1 As mentioned in Chapter Four, to qualify for capital treatment the motive behind the purchase has to be either to finance the payment of inheritance tax on a death, or to benefit the trade being carried on by the company or any of its 75% subsidiaries. This latter test raises a number of questions including:

1 what is the trade?
2 is the trade being carried on?
3 does the benefit arise to the trade?
4 how does the trade benefit?

WHAT IS THE TRADE?

8.2 Short of reciting the Badges of Trade[1] so beloved of tax examiners, a trade can be likened unto the proverbial elephant; we know it when we see it but cannot define it with any accuracy. Whilst the tax legislation in general and the purchase of own shares legislation in particular do not contain any definition of what a trade is, we are at least told what a trade is not. Excluded activities are dealing in shares, securities, land or futures.[2] These are the same activities which are regarded as being beyond the pale for a number of tax provisions, such as inheritance tax business property relief and capital gains tax reinvestment relief, on the basis that they could be closer to being investment activities than trading. It will be those activities on the fringes of trading, largely centred upon land and property, that will create the main problems in this area.

Land and property

8.3 The Revenue have always resisted classifying the generation of rental income from the management of let property as a trade. Thus in the 1982 case of *Gittos v Barclay*[3], where two holiday properties were rented out during the

1 The Royal Commission on the Taxation of Profits and Income 1955 Cmd 9474 para 116.
2 TA 1988 s 229(1).
3 (1982) 55 TC 640.

summer season and actively managed by the taxpayer, he unsuccessfully claimed that the loss that had arisen should be treated as a trading loss. The claim was on the basis of his own and his wife's active involvement in preparing and cleaning the properties at the beginning and end of the season, advertising and dealing with bookings. The court relied upon an earlier decision in *Salisbury House Estate Ltd v Fry*[1] and, in particular, the words of Lord Macmillan who said:

> 'A landowner may conduct a trade on his premises, but he cannot be represented as carrying on a trade of owning land because he makes an income by letting it.'[2]

8.4 Later in 1982, the same question came before the High Court in *Griffiths v Jackson.*[3] A chartered accountant owned a number of properties which were let furnished on short-term tenancies to students and tourists. He claimed that the profits were assessable under Schedule D Case I rather than, as the Revenue contended, Case VI. The significance in those days was that if the income were assessable under Case VI then it would have been liable to the 'investment income surcharge', an additional 15% levy on investment income. In finding for the Revenue, Vinelott J, whilst expressing some sympathy for the taxpayer, quoted Lord Macmillan's remarks in the *Salisbury House* case and then quoted with approval the words of Lord Greene MR in *Sywell Aerodrome Ltd v Croft*:[4]

> '. . . why and on what principle is a person who, for example, sets up a refreshment stall on his land or provides services for people admitted to his land, not exhaustively taxed under Schedule A or B (as the case may be) in respect of the profits so earned? Such a person in my view is not exploiting his rights of occupation save in the sense and to the limited extent that he must own or occupy the land before he can erect and carry on the refreshment stall or perform the services. The profits earned in such a case are referable, not to the rights of property or of occupation since the customers come on to the land for the purpose of obtaining refreshment or procuring the benefit of the services. If, on the other hand, the owner of land having (let me suppose) a remarkable view or some historic monument merely allows the public to come onto the land in return for an admission fee, I cannot myself see why it should be said that his profits are not covered by the Schedule A assessment since all that he is doing is to exploit his right of property by granting licences to come upon the land. The fact that he keeps the paths in order or the monument in repair in order to make a visit more attractive to the public again appears to me to make no difference, any more than does the action of the landlord of a house in keeping it in repair.'

8.5 Thus the hotel proprietor derives income from the carrying on of a trade on his property by the provision of services, such as meals and cleaning the rooms, in addition to allowing use of the rooms to their guests. A landlord of let property, on the other hand, derives income from the exploitation of his or her rights of property and, generally, gives no other services. In conclusion Vinelott J added:

---

1 (1929) 15 TC 266.
2 (1930) 15 TC at p 330.
3 (1982) 56 TC 583.
4 (1941) 24 TC 126.

> 'It is a peculiar feature of United Kingdom tax law that the activity of letting furnished flats or rooms, while it may be a business and, in this case, a demanding and time-consuming business, is not a trade.'[1]

8.6 A trade cannot therefore comprise the mere passive ownership of income-producing property. There must be some activity if a trade is to be established. However, if that activity is solely in respect of the managing the property, rather than the provision of services or goods, it will not assist such a claim. In *Webb v Conelee Properties Ltd*[2] the point at issue was whether the company was a trading or an investment company. It acquired properties and granted licences to occupy to third parties. The company relied heavily upon the scale of activities claimed to have been undertaken in managing the properties. Warner J was not impressed, after mentioning the authorities to which he had been referred, he continued;

> 'It was I think common ground between counsel that those authorities establish that the owner of land may carry on activities on the land that go beyond the mere exploitation of his proprietary rights in the land and which constitute a trade. Where it is shown that there have been such activities, it is a matter of fact and degree whether they are sufficient to amount to the carrying on of a trade.
>
> Council for the Crown submits that, in the present case, it does not appear that the taxpayer company carried on on its properties any activity, such as the provision of services or equipment, capable of constituting a trade. I think he is right.'[3]

and later added,

> 'It seems to me, however, that counsel for the Crown was right when he said that mere management activity was not an activity that was capable of giving rise to the existence of a trade, and that the degree or amount of that activity made no difference so long as it was only management.'[4]

8.7 In 1984 legislation was introduced which enabled income from furnished holiday lettings to be classed as a trade for the purposes of certain tax provisions.[5] Unfortunately none of these provisions is concerned with the purchase of own shares. Therefore capital treatment can never be obtained[6] for a purchase of own shares by a company whose sole activity is furnished holiday lettings, because it has no trade.

8.8 Where, however, the business activity consists of operating a caravan park, including the letting of furnished caravans, this may in fact be a trade within Case I. In a parliamentary reply in 1984, the then Financial Secretary to the Treasury said:

> 'The letting of caravans is regarded as an activity of leasing chattels which may amount to a trade if it is on a sufficient scale and organised and operated on a commercial basis. This can only be determined on the facts

---

1 56 TC at p 593.
2 [1982] STC 913, 56 TC 149.
3 [1982] STC 919h, 56 TC 156H.
4 [1982] STC 920b, 56 TC 157E.
5 TA 1988 s 503.
6 At least not under TA 1988 s 219(1)(a); capital treatment could however be possible where purchase was to fund an IHT liability on a death.

of each case and there can be no hard and fast rule of general application. Where the scale, organisation and operation is such that it does amount to a trade, the income is assessable under Case I of Schedule D; in other cases under Case VI.

Income from letting pitches, that is site rents, is assessable under Schedule A to the extent that it arises from exploiting an interest in land. However, where the provision of associated services assessable under Case I of Schedule D, such as, for example, shops, accounts for a substantial part of the income, in practice the whole income will be included in the Case I computation.'[1]

IS THE TRADE BEING CARRIED ON?

Cessation of trade

8.9 Assuming that there is no problem in the activities being carried on by the company being regarded as a trade, the next step is to ensure that the trade is a continuing one. The Revenue will only agree to capital treatment if the trade is being 'carried on'. It can hardly be said to be of a benefit to the company's trade to purchase those shares if that trade is going to be discontinued in any event. Therefore such treatment will not be available where, for example, the company has sold off its trade, and some shareholders wish to realise their shareholdings by means of a purchase of own shares financed by the sale proceeds. This would be despite the fact that the company may nevertheless use the remaining funds to acquire a new trade.

8.10 The case of a cessation needs to be contrasted with that in *IRC v Patrick Thomson Ltd.*[2] In that case a compensation payment to a director was allowed where the trade was 'hived up' to a parent company and the company itself was liquidated. It was significant that the trade was to continue under the ownership of a different company within the same group rather than be discontinued. The trade was regarded as having an existence independent of the company which, at any point in time, might be carrying on that trade. The judgment of Lord Sorn[3] relied upon passages from the judgments in *Morgan v Tate & Lyle Ltd*,[4] including:

> '. . . it is not difficult to suppose a case where a trader is shortly to be succeeded in his trade by another person and where he spends money the benefit of which will accrue in whole or in part to his successor. It could not be said that for that reason the money was not wholly and exclusively laid out for the purposes of the trade'.[5]
>
> 'Although "the trade" within the meaning of rule 3(a)[6] is no doubt the trade which the Company was carrying on when the sum in question was

1 Inland Revenue Press Release 17 May 1984.
2 (1956) 37 TC 145 (see also para 10.30).
3 (1956) 37 TC at p 162.
4 (1953) 35 TC 367.
5 Lord Reid, (1954) 35 TC at p 423.
6 Rule 3(a) applicable to Cases I and II of Schedule D, First Schedule, Income Tax Act 1918 – now TA 1988 s 74(a).

spent, yet the trade of a company or of any other trader is regarded by the Income Tax Acts as being an entity which can continue to exist notwithstanding that its ownership itself is transferred from one company or person to another company or person.'[1]

'Income tax legislation has at different times made different provisions for cases of discontinuance of a trade or succession to a trade. These are no doubt provisions relating to the manner or measure of assessment, but as they are a clear recognition of common commercial experience of a business continuing through several hands, they indicate that "the trade", when used in the statutes, is to be construed as an entity itself.'[2]

Lord Sorn then concluded:

'. . . it seems to me that the money was expended "wholly and exclusively for the purposes of the trade" and that it did not cease to be so expended because part of the benefit would be enjoyed by the successor.'[3]

Sale of trade

8.11 If by purchasing the shares of a troublesome shareholder, the company was then able to sell its existing trade to another unconnected company which had the capital necessary to inject into that trade and so extend and expand it, would that purchase rank for capital treatment? Whilst it could be argued that the trade had benefited by being under new ownership and thereby new management, the Revenue would probably argue that the benefit arising was the company being able to sell its trade (and perhaps realise a capital gain) which was the sole motive behind the purchase of own shares. Indeed, it is difficult to see how a company could be justified in taking steps designed to ensure that a benefit arises to a trade which is shortly to belong to some other unconnected company unless it was with a view to generating a profit from the disposal.

DOES THE BENEFIT ARISE TO THE TRADE?

8.12 It should also be remembered that not only must there be a motive to benefit the trade, but there must, in addition, be an absence of any motive enabling the shareholder to benefit from the company's profits without receiving a dividend and also an absence of any tax avoidance motive. It is clear that the benefit being sought must arise to the trade and not solely to the company owning the trade. The phrase 'for the purposes of the trade'[4] has been considered by the courts on many occasions and perhaps some guidance on the trading benefit test can be drawn from the decision in *Mallalieu v Drummond*[5] where Lord Brightman said:

---

1 Lord Morton, (1954) 35 TC at p 413.
2 Lord Keith, (1954) 35 TC at p 429.
3 (1956) 37 TC at p 162.
4 TA 1988 s 74(a).
5 [1983] STC 665.

> 'The words in the paragraph[1] "expended for the purposes of the trade, profession or vocation" mean in my opinion "to serve the purposes of the trade, profession or vocation" or as elaborated by Lord Davey in *Strong & Co of Romsey Ltd v Woodifield (Surveyor of Taxes)*[2] "for the purpose of enabling a person to carry on and earn profits in the trade etc." The particular words emphasised do not refer to "the purposes" of the taxpayer as some of the cases appear to suggest . . . they refer to "the purposes" of the business which is a different concept although the "purposes" (ie the intentions or objects) of the taxpayer are fundamental to the application of the paragraph.'

8.13 Putting this into the context of the trading benefit test for a purchase of own shares is not easy but leads to the conclusion that, whilst a benefit may arise for the company, the benefit should be attributable to its trading activities, not to any investment activities. This would seem to be the basis for the Revenue view that the test will not be satisfied where 'the intended benefit for the company is some non-trading activity which it also carries on'.[3]

HOW DOES THE TRADE BENEFIT?

8.14 At first sight it might be asked how the purchase of shares from a shareholder can possibly benefit the trade which, after all, is under the day to day control of the directors not the shareholders? To answer that question requires consideration of four possible scenarios according to the category of the vendor shareholder:

1 the dissident shareholder/director who is seeking to withdraw from involvement with the company as a result of some disagreement;
2 the 'unwilling' or 'disinterested' shareholder who is not also a director. He or she may have become a shareholder by inheritance, gift, or operation of law and have no other particular involvement in the company;
3 the outside equity investor who may also be a director and is now seeking to withdraw his or her investment;
4 the retiring shareholder/director, perhaps the founder or major shareholder.

The dissident shareholder/director

8.15 The case for the removal of such a director may be thought to be self-evident. However, could not that benefit be achieved by simply removing that individual from his or her position as a director (assuming there were grounds for such action) without the necessity of purchasing their shares? In an extreme case perhaps that is possible, but often companies will want to achieve a negotiated withdrawal. A sale of the individual's shareholding will

1 TA 1988 s 74(a).
2 (1905) 5 TC 215.
3 Statement of Practice SP2/82, para 1.

be part of the conditions for his or her departure. Not only will the company be reluctant to retain a dissident shareholder, the individual will not tolerate an investment in a company over whose affairs he has no control. Viewed in that light it is clear that a trading benefit must arise out of the removal of a dissident shareholder/director, and this, as indicated earlier, must clearly involve a complete parting of the ways.

8.16 The Statement of Practice appearing in the new version of Booklet IR131, published in July 1994, was a completely re-written version. No explanation was given by the Revenue for the reason for the re-write nor whether this implied a change of policy. One notable omission from the current version concerns the question of shareholders' disagreements. In the original version a non-qualifying example was given of a disagreement over whether the company should continue trading and become an investment company and the departing shareholder was one who advocated the continuance of trading. If, on the other hand, the dissident was pressing for a cessation of the trade, then by implication, the purchase would qualify for capital treatment.

The unwilling shareholder

8.17 It is perhaps more difficult to see how the removal of an unwilling, rather than a dissident, shareholder (who perhaps is not a director) can benefit the trade, especially where the holding concerned is, say, less than 25%. If they are in such a position, they cannot really be said to prejudice the ongoing trading activities of the company.[1] The Revenue, however, apply a much more liberal approach. They offer as examples of situations where a trading benefit would be regarded as arising, the legatee or personal representatives of a deceased shareholder who have no desire to retain them. Originally they accepted that it would be 'unsatisfactory to retain an unwilling shareholder'[2] without actually explaining the reasons why. Later they explained that the unwilling shareholder might sell his or her shares to someone who was unacceptable to the continuing shareholders.[3] Despite this explanation it remains difficult to see a direct link between the identity of minority shareholders and the fortunes of the company's trading activities.

8.18 It might be thought that an alternative defence would be for the directors to exercise an absolute power under the company's Articles[4] to refuse to register any transfer of shares to an 'undesirable'. However where such a right is exercised, it does not deprive the transferee of his or her beneficial ownership. The transferor will remain on the register of members, and will be a bare trustee able to exercise votes on behalf of the transferee.

1 Except perhaps if they were to petition the court that the company's affairs were being conducted in a manner which was unfairly prejudicial to his or her interests. But then, of course, they would become 'dissident'.
2 Original version of Statement of Practice SP 2/82, para 4.
3 Current version of Statement of Practice SP 2/82, para 2.
4 This must be under the company's Articles as regulation 24 of the 1985 version of Table A only gives a limited power to refuse to register a transfer. However some companies will have adopted the 1948 version of Table A which empowers directors to refuse to register *any* transfer without giving reasons – Companies Act 1948 Sch 1 Part II reg 3.

The outside equity investor

8.19 Statement of Practice SP2/82 (current version) treats this category as 'unwilling' and if the purpose is to prevent those shares falling into the wrong hands, it will be accepted that a trading benefit arises. Those investors will have had to satisfy the five-year ownership test. It is logical that any profit made by them should be accorded capital treatment. After all, by their original investment they have put capital at risk for at least that period. The profit is not a short-term profit and should not be taxed as such. This logic is not sufficient to satisfy the trading benefit test. A purist may argue that the trade will, or should have, benefited from the original capital injection and cannot benefit from the repayment of that capital and its appreciation.

8.20 The unwilling shareholder can perhaps be contrasted with the equity investor in that the latter will probably be an influential minority holder who will have a considerable nuisance value if he or she becomes 'dissident'.

The retiring shareholder/director

8.21 The Revenue accept that a trading benefit would arise where the controlling shareholder[1] is retiring to make way for new management. He or she would have been involved in the management of the company's trade and presumably the thinking is that the trade will benefit from his or her departure to make way for new blood. There would seem to be an obvious benefit to the trade even though this might not be obvious to the departing shareholder! The advantage to the trade is not perhaps that the departing shareholder was damaging the trade, but more that it must be advantageous to allow for an orderly succession to, and continuation of, the trade. If shareholders were not able to sell their shares back to the company, and could not find another purchaser, they might liquidate the company in order to realise their investment. Thus, by allowing a purchase of own shares, the trade benefits by remaining in being.

---

1 Described as simply 'the founder' in the original version.

Chapter Nine

THE SUBSTANTIAL REDUCTION AND CONNECTION TESTS

MARRIED COUPLES AS THE ONLY SHAREHOLDERS

9.1 In order to qualify for capital treatment the vendor must not be connected with the company immediately after the purchase or redemption.[1] Furthermore, in order to satisfy the trading benefit test[2] it will often be necessary for a retiring shareholder/director to dispose of his or her entire shareholding.

9.2 Where a working spouse is standing down from active management in the company, the question of succession will arise. Some of the shares may have to find their way into the hands of the next generation of shareholders, whether these are other family members or the existing management. The complication here in connection with a purchase or redemption is that a company cannot simply disappear into thin air by buying back all its shares; some irredeemable shares must remain in issue.[3] Any shares retained by the other spouse would be held by an associate of the vendor and therefore regarded as the vendor's for the purposes of the connection test.[4] The effect of this attribution is that the vendor will still be regarded as holding 100% of the issued share capital. Therefore the purchase would not qualify for capital treatment and any retirement relief which might otherwise be available would be wasted.

9.3 In such a situation what is needed is a third shareholder who does not fall within the definition of an 'associate'.[5] The obvious candidate is an adult child of the vendor, if such a person exists. A transfer to such a person must be an outright gift and not the creation of a trust, as the trustees would be associates of the settlor.[6] If a suitable recipient of shares can be found, the question of how and when to transfer those shares is crucial. Because retirement relief, except in ill-health cases, is given automatically if all the conditions are satisfied, the gift before the purchase by the company would unnecessarily attract retirement relief which might be required on the subsequent purchase. On the other hand, if the gift were delayed until after the

1 Para 4.14.
2 Para 4.12.
3 CA 1985 s 162(3).
4 TA 1988 s 221(2).
5 See para 4.16.
6 TA 1988 s 227(5).

purchase, the vendor may have failed to achieve a substantial reduction and/or may still be connected with the company.

9.4 With advance planning, of course, it would be possible to make the gift to the adult child on the day before the vendor's 50th birthday and claim hold-over relief.[1] However such situations arise only in the tax-planner's mind, not in reality. A more convoluted way around the problem needs to be found. What is required is a transfer of shares from the vendor without triggering a disposal. This requires the use of the spouse exemption because a transfer to the non-working spouse does not give rise to any gain, therefore no retirement relief is wasted. A gift from the non-working spouse to the adult child will also not involve the loss of any retirement relief as that spouse was, by definition, not entitled to retirement relief anyway. That transfer can be the subject of a hold-over claim.

Example

Jim holds 600 shares out of 1,000 in issue. His wife, Ethel, holds the remaining 400. They have an adult son, Neddie. Jim is 50 years of age and wishes to realise capital from the company which can only realistically fund a purchase price of £250,000, which is the market value of a holding of 400 shares. The conditions with regard to retirement relief are satisfied in relation to Jim but not Ethel. Similarly, all conditions for capital treatment would be satisfied if Jim's entire shareholding were to be sold.

9.5 The dilemma is, what is to happen to Jim's surplus 200 shares?

1. If he retains them, the Revenue are unlikely to accept that a benefit to the trade would arise from the purchase. In any event Jim will fail the substantial reduction test as he and his associate, Ethel, will still hold 100% of the issued share capital. He will also fail the connection test for the same reason.
2. If he gives them to Neddie *after* the purchase, he will also fail the substantial reduction and connection tests as these must be satisfied *immediately after* the purchase by the company.
3. If he gives them to Neddie *before* the purchase, he will have wasted some retirement relief on that disposal. This is because retirement relief, except on ill-health grounds, is given automatically if all the conditions are satisfied. The effect would be that Neddie would benefit from the retirement relief by having a base cost equal to market value at the date of gift, but this is not perhaps what Jim had in mind! (Of course, if Jim is unlikely to be able to utilise all his available relief, this will not be a problem.)
4. If he gifts them to Ethel before the sale, then the situation is as in (1) above, BUT if, also before the purchase by the company, Ethel were to gift 421 shares to Neddie, she would end up owning 179 out of 600 in issue, which is just under 30% and Jim would satisfy the connection test. Because, after the purchase, Jim will not hold any shares in the company, the substantial reduction test is not applicable.

1 TCGA 1992 s 165.

9.6 The Revenue are, however, on record as saying that where inter-spouse transfers are made as part of arrangements leading to a purchase of own shares, they would deny capital treatment on the grounds that this indicated a scheme whose main purpose was the avoidance of tax.[1] The need for advance planning is clear. If the transfer to the spouse had taken place some time earlier, as part of an overall re-arrangement of their respective estates and before a purchase of own shares had even been contemplated, a valid defence should be available.

GIFTING TO THE COMPANY

9.7 The general prohibition on a company acquiring its own shares is not only relaxed to enable it to purchase or redeem its shares within the framework described in Chapter Two, but also to enable it to acquire any of its fully paid shares 'otherwise than for valuable consideration'.[2] In other words, it may receive a gift of its own shares.

9.8 Unlike a purchase or redemption, there is no provision requiring shares received by way of a gift to be cancelled. Therefore the company becomes a member of itself. This raises a number of interesting questions as far as taxation is concerned, not least being how this phenomenon could be of use in the context of a purchase of own shares. Firstly, however, it is necessary to consider the mechanism for perfecting such a gift.

The theory

9.9 The gift itself can be carried out by executing a share transfer in favour of the company and the transfer will be exempt from stamp duty,[3] the certificate on the back of the form being completed to show that the transaction falls within item L as a voluntary inter vivos disposition.

9.10 An intriguing question is whether a company could end up owning its entire issued share capital by means of such a gift and a purchase and cancellation of the remaining shares. The previous obstacle, that at least two members of a company were required, no longer exists. Following the purchase of own shares there would still be some irredeemable shares in issue, albeit held by the company itself, so the purchase could be valid. It is difficult to see how the company could be voluntarily wound up in that there would be no ordinary shareholder left to whom any surplus could be distributed. The concept of a memberless private company was something of a Holy Grail in the days of apportionment of a close company's relevant income. Presumably as the gifted shares remain in being they could be sold by the company if necessary to unscramble the situation. Alternatively there would be no reason why the company could not issue new shares to future members.

1 TA 1988 s 219(1)(a).
2 CA 1985 s 143(3).
3 The Stamp Duty (Exempt Instruments) Regulations 1987 SI 1987 No 516.

Practical uses

9.11 In the context of a purchase of own shares, a gift of shares could take the place of the gift by Ethel to Neddie in the example quoted at paragraph **9.5**. The question which then arises is whether the company is an associate of Jim. Certainly it would be if Jim were connected with the company[1] but he cannot be within the definition of 'connection' for these purposes as he and his associate only hold 179 shares out of the 600 still in issue, (29.83%). In addition, because Jim has sold all his shares to the company, the substantial reduction test is not applicable.[2]

9.12 It may also be the case that the company cannot raise the finance to purchase the entire holding or that it would be imprudent to do so. Again, what is needed if the retiring shareholder is to obtain capital treatment is that the balance of his or her shares must be transferred to someone who is not an associate. Whilst the possibility exists of transferring the surplus shares to an adult child, subject to the limitations set out in paragraph **9.5**, there may be situations where that is not possible. The alternatives include a sale to a third party or the remaining shareholders, or if all else fails, gifting the shares to the company itself.

9.13 The difference would be that shares gifted remain in being whereas shares sold have to be cancelled. As the Revenue accept that a company does not make an acquisition by a purchase, it is not possible to claim capital gains tax hold over relief[3] on the gain as this requires there to be both a disposal and an acquisition. This is likely to be treated as a transaction 'otherwise than at arm's length' and therefore treated as taking place at market value.[4]

9.14 However, with a gift there is clearly an acquisition. There would therefore seem to be little or no tax liability involved in making a gift of shares to the company. If the company is a trading company (and it would need to be for the purchase of own shares to be eligible for capital treatment) there is no reason why a claim could not be made to holdover the capital gain on that disposal. Such a claim has to be made by the transferor and 'the person who acquires the asset' which, of course, is the company. In the context of a purchase of own shares, the Revenue accept that for the purposes of relief for any capital loss arising under the distribution treatment, the company does not acquire the shares on the grounds that the shares are cancelled upon completion of the purchase. In the case of a gift to the company no cancellation occurs, therefore the shares remain in existence and the company must have made an acquisition.

9.15 At first sight it might be thought that for inheritance tax purposes the gift of shares must be a transfer of value, on which tax would be chargeable subject to the annual exemption and the availability of the nil rate band. This view would be on the assumption that the gift could not qualify as a

1 TA 1988 s 227(3).
2 Para 4.24.
3 TCGA 1992 s 165.
4 TCGA 1992 s 17(1)(b).

potentially exempt transfer because those are generally outright gifts to individuals. However, whilst the legislation does require a potentially exempt transfer to be a gift to another individual[1] it further provides that a transfer is regarded as a gift to an individual, where, even though the property gifted does not become comprised in the donee's estate, the value of the estate of another individual is increased.[2]

9.16 Of course, if a sole shareholder were to gift some of his or her holding to the company, there would actually be no transfer of value because there would be no loss in value of his or her estate. Where there are two or more individual shareholders then there will be some loss in value to the transferor's estate. If the only other individual shareholder is the spouse of the transferor, then, whilst his or her estate will have been increased, it is possible to rely upon the inter-spouse exemption to cover that transfer. In order to be within the exemption either the property gifted has to become comprised in the spouse's estate or the value of that estate has to be increased as a result of that transfer.[3]

SATISFYING THE TESTS

9.17 The substantial reduction test only comes into play where the vendor does not sell the whole of his or her shareholding. In most cases where a founder shareholder wishes to withdraw from the business or where a dissident shareholder wishes to be bought out, the intention will be to dispose of the whole holding. In other cases, however, this may not be possible and the substantial reduction test may make the difference between capital treatment and distribution treatment.

Example

Wallace holds 50 shares, the trustees of a settlement he created hold 250 and Albert, his son, the remaining 700 shares. If the company purchases the whole of Wallace's holding, the holding of his associates becomes 250 out of 950 in issue (26.31%) so he is not connected with the company. The substantial reduction test is not in point and therefore, if all other conditions are satisfied, the purchase will be eligible for capital treatment.

However, if Wallace only sells 49 shares, the substantial reduction test will apply and the rights of himself and his associates fall from 30% (300 out of 1,000) to 26.39% (251 out of 951) so that the connection test is satisfied. This is a reduction of only 12% and the substantial reduction test is therefore not satisfied. The distribution treatment therefore applies to the purchase.

1 IHTA 1984 s 3A(1)(c).
2 IHTA 1984 s 3A(2)(b).
3 IHTA 1984 s 18(1).

9.18 This is an extreme example but serves to illustrate the point. In cases where this kind of situation applies, what is required is for the associate to reduce his or her holding at the same time. This could be a gift to a member of the family who is not an associate of the vendor (Neddie of paragraph **9.5**), a gift to the company or a sale to the company. In the latter case the associate would automatically be regarded as satisfying the substantial reduction and connection tests even if they would not otherwise do so, provided that he or she was only selling the shares to enable the 'main' vendor to satisfy the substantial reduction test.[1] All the other tests however, would need to be satisfied.

Partial purchases

9.19 Situations may often arise where the company cannot fund an outright purchase and may have to proceed on the basis of a purchase in two or more tranches. Capital treatment will be prejudiced by such steps as the vendor may fail to satisfy the substantial reduction test on all but the last tranche. He or she may also remain connected with the company by the possession of more than 30% of the loan and share capital or the possession of more than 30% of the voting power.

9.20 Company law requires the proceeds to be paid in full on completion[2] so that it is not possible to have a purchase of the entire shareholding and leave the purchase price outstanding. To do so would not be a valid purchase of own shares and apart from the legal complications the Revenue would not grant capital treatment to the transaction.[3] What is permissible is for all the shares to be sold, the company to pay the purchase price in full and for the vendor to make an immediate loan back to the company. This overcomes the company law problem but still leaves the possibility that the vendor might remain connected by possessing more than 30% of the loan and share capital, particularly if the company only had a small share capital.

9.21 One possibility which has been suggested to cope with this scenario is the use of a single purchase contract for the whole of the shares but completion to take place in tranches over a period of time. The thinking is that as the single unconditional purchase contract is sufficient to deprive the vendor of his or her beneficial ownership in the shares, this will satisfy the substantial reduction test. In addition, as payment for each tranche will be made on completion of that tranche, the company law requirement will be satisfied. Further, as the company is not indebted to the vendor for any part of the purchase price, which only becomes due on completion, the vendor will not possess more than 30% of the share and loan capital and will not therefore be connected.

9.22 A problem still exists, however, with regard to voting rights. Part of the connection test is that the vendor must not directly or indirectly possess or be

---

1 TA 1988 s 224.
2 CA 1985 s 159(3).
3 In fact it would probably give rise to a liability under TA 1988 s 419 on the amount actually paid out.

entitled to acquire more than 30% of the voting power in the company.[1] During the period from the date of the unconditional contract to the date of completion the vendor will continue to be the legal owner of the shares but as trustee for the company. The vendor will remain on the Register of Members in respect of those shares and will be in a position to exercise the votes attaching to them; the question is whether he or she will therefore 'possess' that voting power. It seems clear from case law that the transferee, in this case the company itself, would only be able to direct the vendor how to vote if the purchase price had been paid over.[2] If in this period between contract and completion, the vendor can exercise voting rights without reference to the company, then he or she may well be connected with the company by the possession of voting power.

9.23 Although it would be only natural to think that voting power must go hand in hand with beneficial ownership, there are precedents in case law to the contrary. In the years following the Second World War a number of cases came before the courts in respect of Excess Profits Tax which had been introduced at the start of that conflict. Under that regime it was advantageous to show that a company was not one in which the directors had a 'controlling interest'. In the case of *IRC v J. Bibby & Sons Ltd*[3] the directors personally held less than 50% of the issued ordinary share capital. However, three of the directors who were brothers were also trustees of their sister's marriage settlement. As such they held further shares which, if added to their personal holdings would have been sufficient to give them more than 50% of the voting power. In the House of Lords it was held that voting power as a trustee was to be taken into account. 'A controlling interest' was 'the power by the exercise of voting rights to carry a resolution at a general meeting of the company':

> 'Those who by their votes control the company do not the less control the company because they may themselves be amenable to some external control. Theirs is the control, though in the exercise of it they may be guilty of some breach of obligation, whether of conscience or of law.'[4]

9.24 This decision was followed in *IRC v Silverts Ltd*[5] where a similar point arose in relation to national defence contribution (later re-named, profits tax'). In finding for the company in the Court of Appeal, Sir Raymond Evershead MR said:

> 'In our judgement the ratio decidendi in *Bibby's* case is that in accordance with well-established principles relating to limited companies a question of the rights of members *vis-à-vis* the corporation (such as voting control under its regulations) is to be determined by reference, and by reference only, to the share register, beyond which it is not (save possibly in the case of mere "nominee" shareholders) permissible to look; and not that in the case of a trust the powers and discretions of exercising votes in regard to shares must be treated as reposing in the trustees without regard to the terms of the trust or the right of the beneficiaries to direct such exercise.'[6]

1 TA 1988 s 228(2)(c).
2 *Musselwhite v C H Musselwhite & Son Ltd* [1962] 1 All ER 201.
3 (1943) 29 TC 167.
4 Lord Simonds, (1943) 29 TC at p 184.
5 (1950) 29 TC 491.
6 (1951) 29 TC at pp 507 to 508.

9.25 It seems clear therefore that the vendor of shares remains in possession of voting power for the period from contract to completion, despite having lost beneficial ownership. If those shares represent more than 30% of the voting power of the company then he or she will remain connected with the company. It is also clear that the vendor could not seek to avoid connection in a partial sale situation by transferring the unsold shares to a nominee or bare trustee. Apart from the fact that the comments in the *Silverts* case quoted above suggest that it is permissible to look behind nominees and bare trustees, the shareholder would clearly have a right to have the shares transferred back into his or her name. Therefore he or she would be 'entitled to acquire'[1] the voting rights attaching to those shares and would remain connected.

9.26 The Revenue are on record as stating that in the case where a vendor shareholder loans back some or all of the purchase price to the company because it cannot afford to pay in full, there will be no objection to the making of a bonus issue to the remaining shareholders in order to prevent the vendor from being connected.[2] Such a bonus issue would have to be made before the purchase takes place to ensure that 'immediately after' the purchase the vendor was not connected. In addition, the company would need to have sufficient distributable reserves to cover the bonus issue; the purchase itself could be out of capital. At the same time those reserves need to be represented by illiquid assets, eg property as the shortage of cash is the reason why the company is not purchasing the vendor's shareholding in its entirety. It also needs to be remembered that a bonus issue will have implications for any future purchases or redemptions.[3]

9.27 Given that the sole object behind such a bonus issue is merely to satisfy the connection test for the vendor, and thus reduce his or her tax liability, it is a little surprising that it should be publicised by the Revenue and for them to state that this will not prejudice capital treatment. After all, is it not 'part of a scheme or arrangement . . . one of the main purposes of which is . . . the avoidance of tax'?[4] If there is a provision of the Taxes Acts that the Revenue feel disposed to suggest ways of circumventing, it may be asked why they do not simply repeal or amend that provision.

Simultaneous purchases

9.28 If two shareholders wish to withdraw from the company at the same time, the application of the substantial reduction and connection tests can have some anomalous results. These arise from the requirement that the tests need to be satisfied 'immediately after the purchase'.

---

1 TA 1988 s 228(2).
2 *Inland Revenue Tax Bulletin* No 21 February 1996.
3 See para 3.6.
4 TA 1988 s 219(1)(b).

Example

Warwick Ltd has an issued share capital of 3,000 ordinary shares which have been held equally for many years by three brothers Richard, John and Harry. The eldest two, Richard and John are over 50 years old and wish to retire and sell their shares. Harry cannot afford to buy their shares and the company, at this stage, can only afford to buy 700 shares in total. Richard and John agree that they will each sell 350 shares to the company and will sell the balance at some point in the future when the company is in a better financial position. In view of paragraph 5 of Statement of Practice SP2/82, the Revenue can be expected to agree that the purchases would be for the benefit of the trade.

If Richard's shares were to be purchased first, his holding would fall from 1,000 out of 3,000 (33.3%) to 650 out of 2,650 (24.5%), a reduction of 26.4%, so that the substantial reduction test would be satisfied.

When John's shares were subsequently purchased, his holding would fall from 1,000 out of 2,650 (37.7%) to 650 out of 2,300 (28.2%), a reduction of 25.2%, so, again, the substantial reduction test would be satisfied.

However, if both purchases were to be dealt with by the same resolution and same contract, then it seems that each brother would fail the test. Each holding would fall from 33.3% to 28.2%, a reduction of only 15.3%.

It should be noticed that John's percentage shareholding increased from 33.3% to 37.7% as a result of the purchase and cancellation of Richard's shares. It is only this increase which enables him to meet the substantial reduction test; combining the purchases into one transaction has deprived John of this advantage.

9.29 There are probably endless permutations of this kind of situation. These illustrate that the order in which purchases are made, or whether they are made as one transaction, could have a significant effect on whether the substantial reduction or the connection tests are satisfied. The moral, however, is a simple one; there is really no alternative but to sit down and perform the calculations.

Chapter Ten

Ancillary Tax Issues

VALUATION

10.1 So far in this work it has been assumed that the purchase or redemption concerned will be carried out at market value. But what is 'market value' and what are the consequences of a purchase or redemption above or below market value?

10.2 At the outset it needs to be appreciated that nowhere in the purchase of own shares legislation is it specified that the purchase should be at market value. Company law is solely concerned with the protection of creditors. Provided that their interests are not prejudiced and the remaining shareholders are content, there is no legal limitation upon the price which can be paid.

10.3 The question therefore arises as to what extent the Revenue consider the purchase price of the shares in granting clearance for capital treatment. The published Revenue Manuals do not include those relating to specialist departments such as Company Tax Division 2 which deals with clearances. However, as they have only 30 days to respond, there is little time available to consider the level of the price to be paid, given that this would presumably involve a reference to Shares Valuation Division who are not renowned for their expedition. However, it is known that, because the capital gains tax connected persons provisions[1] do not apply,[2] local Inspectors are instructed not to approach the Division for a valuation on those grounds. They can, however, approach that Division if they believe that the purchase was not a bargain made at arm's length.[3] Basically it appears that the Revenue will not seek to challenge the purchase price unless it seems wildly excessive.

Purchase in excess of market value

10.4 If the purchase is at a price in excess of market value, then there must be a case for the Revenue claiming that a distribution has occurred because the shareholder has received value over and above the value of the shares he

---

1 TCGA 1992 s 18 which requires there to be both an acquisition and a disposal.
2 Because there is no acquisition by the company.
3 Inland Revenue Company Tax Manual CT 58645.

or she has sold.[1] A distribution would arise on the excess of the purchase price over market value even if the purchase satisfied all the tests for capital treatment. Obviously, if the distribution treatment is required, the level of the purchase price will be uncontentious as that treatment will apply to the whole of the consideration.

Purchase at less than market value

Inheritance Tax

10.5 If the purchase price were to be less than market value, then prima facie there would be a transfer of value for inheritance tax purposes by the vendor. The main defence for such a proposition would be to maintain that the transaction was not intended to confer any gratuitous benefit.[2]

10.6 In order to mount a successful defence, the vendor in this type of situation will have to surmount a number of hurdles. He or she will have to show that all of the following three conditions are satisfied:

1 that there was no intention of conferring any benefit on anyone.[3] In simple terms, they would have to show that they simply made a 'bad bargain', but at the time of the transaction they believed that they were receiving full value for the shares. The problem faced by the vendor is, of course, what evidence can be produced to show that lack of intention?

2 either;
 (a) that this was not a transaction between connected persons; or
 (b) that it was such as might have been expected to have been made in a transaction at arms length between unconnected persons.

 Alternative (a) is unlikely to be a possibility in the case of a family controlled company as, even if the vendor is a minority shareholder, he or she will probably be one of a group of people connected with each other who control the company and therefore he or she will be connected with the company.[4] This will leave (b) and the vendor will have to show that those elements which would be present in an arm's length transaction were present in this case. As a minimum it would probably be necessary to show that the vendor and the company were separately advised and that there had been some element of negotiation. This is unlikely to be the case where the purchase is from a majority shareholder;

3 that the price was either 'freely negotiated' or such a price as might be expected to be freely negotiated at the time of the sale. This is an additional condition applicable in the case of unquoted shares and the difference between this and (2) above is not immediately apparent, except that this is concentrated on the price, whereas (2) above is concerned with all the other factors surrounding the transaction.

---

1 TA 1988 s 209(4).
2 IHTA 1984 s 10.
3 IHTA 1984 s 10(1).
4 TCGA 1992 s 286.

10.7 The burden of proof clearly rests on the vendor and in order to avoid any transfer of value occurring every effort should be made to establish a defendable market value for the shares.

Capital gains tax

10.8 Normally a transaction between a company and its shareholders might be expected to be one between connected persons and as such, the capital gains tax computation is based upon market value at the date of disposal rather than the actual consideration.[1] However this rule only applies where there is both a disposal and an acquisition.[2] As the Revenue accept that the company does not acquire the shares being purchased, it cannot apply.

10.9 However, market value can be substituted for the actual consideration where the transaction is one 'otherwise than by way of a bargain at arm's length.'[3] Such a transaction would be one where either the price or some other term was not in line with what might be expected in a freely negotiated transaction between two parties, each attempting to get the best deal for themselves. The Revenue's view is that a transaction is not at arm's length if one party has no intention of getting the best deal[4] and thus intends to confer some benefit on the other. They would be looking at such factors as whether the parties were separately advised and represented, whether there were 'real' negotiations and whether the terms of the transaction were in line with those which might be found in comparable commercial transactions.[5]

10.10 If the Revenue are able to substitute the market value for the proceeds and the resulting capital gain is not covered by any relief, it will not be possible to claim hold-over relief on the 'gift' element of the gain. Relief can only be claimed where there has been an acquisition, and, as mentioned, the Revenue believe that there would be no acquisition by the company.

CONSEQUENCES

10.11 Regardless of the tax treatment, one of the immediate consequences of a purchase or redemption is that the percentage shareholdings of the remaining shareholders will be increased. Although their holdings will be unchanged, the number of shares in issue will be reduced. This could, in turn, lead to a particular shareholder now having a controlling interest which changes the valuation basis of that holding and increases the value of his or her estate. In the context of a purchase carried out by a trading company, this may be felt not to create any tax disadvantage due to the current availability of 100% business property relief from inheritance tax. However, the point may be relevant in the case of an investment company or a trading company

1 TCGA 1992 s 18.
2 TCGA 1992 s 18(1).
3 TCGA 1992 s 17(1)(a).
4 Inland Revenue Capital Gains Manual CG 14542.
5 Inland Revenue Capital Gains Manual CG 14545.

where business property relief is denied because of 'excepted assets' or a failure to satisfy the ownership requirement.

10.12 The increase in the value of the remaining shareholders' estates will come about even though the purchase of the vendor's shares may have been at market value. In such a case this increase will arise solely because the basis of valuation moves from a minority or earnings basis to a majority or assets basis.

Example

Assume the shares in a particular company can be valued as follows:

Percentage Holding	Value per share
	£
below 25%	20
25%–49%	50
50%–74%	100
75% and over	150

and that the shares are held as follows:

	Shares	Value of holding
		£
A	400	20,000
B	400	20,000
C	200	4,000
	1,000	44,000

The first thing to notice is that whilst the company's net assets may be worth £150,000, the combined value of each shareholding taken in isolation, is much less. It does not reflect the 'marriage value' which would arise if all the shares were in the ownership of one person.

If A withdraws from the company, which purchases his entire holding for its market value of £20,000, the net assets of the company will fall to £130,000. The value of C's shareholding, which was previously a 20% holding and worth, on a minority basis, £4,000, will become a 33% holding (200 shares out of 600 in issue). Because this would have the ability to block a special resolution, its unit value will increase to £50 per share. The fact that the company's net assets will drop by £20,000 should not have any effect on that minority value as that will be based upon earnings. The company's future earnings capability should not be affected by the purchase, indeed perhaps it should be improved if the purchase really is for the benefit of the trade.

B's position will be even more dramatically changed. From a 40% holding worth £20,000 on an influential minority basis it will become a controlling 67% holding which is arguably worth say £195[1] per share or £78,000.

1 67% of net asset value of £130,000 less 10% discount.

Effect on future share values

10.13 As far as share valuations in the future are concerned, an interesting question is whether Shares Valuation Division will take into account a purchase of own shares in agreeing a valuation of the company's shares at some subsequent date and whether it received capital or distribution treatment.

10.14 The answer must be that a value is required at a specific point in time. It is the price which a hypothetical prudent purchaser would pay on that date for the holding being valued. An isolated purchase of own shares would be taken into account by a purchaser but only insofar as he would take into account an isolated dividend. There would be no guarantee of recurrence, although the fact that the company had the power to purchase its own shares would be seen as an attraction in that it offers the purchaser another potential buyer for his shares when he comes to realise his investment.

RETIREMENT RELIEF

10.15 Perhaps the main attraction of a purchase of own shares is that it provides retiring shareholders with a method of realising some capital from their investment without the need to find outside purchasers for the shares, or even to place the company into liquidation. It is therefore often the case that a vendor will be at an age where capital gains tax retirement relief will be available. This can be used to shelter the gain which would otherwise arise on the sale of the shares to the company. It is worth remembering the main conditions for retirement relief, which can be summarised as being:

1 the individual must be over 50 years of age[1] or must have retired on ill-health grounds below that age;
2 he or she must also have been a full time officer or employee of the company,[2] which means devoting substantially the whole of his or her time to the service of that company in a managerial or technical capacity;[3]
3 the company must have been the individual's 'personal company'[4], which means he or she must have held at least 5% of the voting rights in the company;
4 the company must be an unquoted trading company or a member of a trading group.[5]

10.16 Conditions (2), (3) and (4) must be satisfied for at least one year up to the date of the sale and for 10 years if the maximum relief is to be available. A point often overlooked is that the test in (3) is by reference to voting rights not to the number of shares held. Therefore, as long as the individual has held at least 5% of the voting rights in the company for the full 10 years, he or she

1 TCGA 1992 s 163(1)(a).
2 TCGA 1992 s 163(5)(b).
3 TCGA 1992 Sch 6 para 1(2).
4 TCGA 1992 s 163(5)(b).
5 TCGA 1992 Sch 6 para 1(2).

will be entitled to full relief on all the shares sold, even if some of those were acquired within the last 10 years.

10.17 In many cases, where a married couple hold shares, one spouse will not be in a position to claim retirement relief. This is usually because they would not satisfy the full-time working officer or employee definition. Clearly if a spouse is a director or employee, but only paid a salary which was just below the national insurance limit, the Revenue may need some convincing that they were working full-time! No doubt there are cases where the remuneration charged in the accounts is not a true reflection of the services provided, but such cases will be few and far between and the Revenue will naturally be sceptical.

10.18 At the same time, the other spouse's entitlement to relief may be in excess of the potential capital gain on his or her shares. In such a case one approach would be to transfer the shares from the non-working spouse to the other. The transfer itself will not be a chargeable event for either capital gains tax or inheritance tax because of the inter-spouse exemptions.[1] Because the transferee spouse only needs to have held 5% of the voting power for the qualifying period, the relief which they have available may cover the gain on the shares transferred from the spouse as well as their original shares.

10.19 Although for capital treatment the shares being sold generally need to have been held for five years, an inter-spouse transfer will not prejudice this test. Provided the parties are still living together at the date of sale, the period of ownership by the transferor is regarded as ownership by the transferee.[2]

COLLATERAL TRANSACTIONS

10.20 The Revenue expect to be informed of any other transactions being entered into with the vendor at or about the same time as the purchase or redemption. Clearance for capital treatment, if granted, will be conditional upon no collateral transactions taking place, other than those disclosed in the clearance application.

Sales of assets

10.21 It has been established that acceptable collateral transactions include sales of company assets to the outgoing shareholder, provided they are at market value. There is, of course, an inherent danger in trying to determine the market value of any asset for which there is no publicly quoted market. The Shares Valuation Division or the District Valuer may always come up with a different figure. If a sale of a company asset has to be part of the deal

1 TCGA 1992 s 58 and IHTA 1984 s 18 (assuming the transferee spouse is domiciled in the UK).
2 TA 1988 s 220(6).

and if capital treatment is desired, then it may be possible for the sales proceeds to be adjusted to the value subsequently agreed by the Revenue.

10.22 In the context of pre-1991 offshore trusts, any additional bounty added by the settlor will 'taint' the trust.[1] The trust will not be tainted by any transaction entered into at arm's length. For these purposes the Revenue will accept that where the contract for the sale contains a provision for 'an appropriate adjustment to the consideration where the value agreed by the Revenue differs from the original consideration arrived at by an independent valuer and specified in the sale document', the transaction is 'in general' regarded as being at arm's length, and thus no bounty would be added to the trust.[2]

10.23 If that principle can apply in one area of taxation, there is no valid reason why it should not apply in the case of the kind of collateral transaction under discussion. Indeed there are instances where such a provision has been accepted as effective for capital gains purposes. Of course, if the vendor required distribution treatment, then a sale of an asset by the company at an undervalue at the same time as the purchase of redemption, would seem to ensure that treatment.

'Golden handshakes'

10.24 Where a shareholder/director is withdrawing from their involvement in the company, it might be suggested, probably by the individual himself, that he should receive a 'golden handshake' as well as selling his shares back to the company. After all, every layman knows that this is a simple way of receiving £30,000 tax free.

10.25 What the layman does not appreciate is that all this has been tried before and that a number of major obstacles exist. The Revenue seem to refuse to give clearance for capital treatment unless the compensation payment is treated as part of the consideration for the shares. The effect of this Revenue view would not only bring the compensation into charge to capital gains tax but also prevent the paying company from claiming a deduction for that sum in calculating its profits liable to corporation tax. The basis for this approach, it is presumed, is that the compensation indicates that the purchase is part of a scheme, one of the main purposes of which is the avoidance of tax.[3] It has also been suggested that the Revenue rely upon the decision in *Bassett Enterprise Ltd v Petty*,[4] a case which deserves close examination.

10.26 The company was controlled by the sons, daughters and a grandson of the founder of the business. The sons, the grandson and the husbands of the daughters were all employed by the company in various capacities. A dispute arose when a prospective purchaser made an offer for the entire issued

1 The Revenue will then be able to assess any capital gains made by the non-resident trustees on the UK resident settlor under TCGA 1992 s 86.
2 Statement of Practice SP5/92.
3 TA 1988 s 219(1)(a)(ii).
4 (1938) 21 TC 730.

share capital and one group of shareholders wished to sell out but the other group refused. They in fact applied for an injunction to prevent the first group from selling. The dispute was finally resolved by both groups agreeing to sell to the purchaser and for those members and husbands of members who were employed by the company to be paid £1,500 each. The company claimed a deduction for these payments. The Special Commissioners found on the evidence presented that the cancellation of the service contracts was part of the share purchase transaction and 'that the expense incurred was not required in the interests of the Company, but in the interests of the purchaser of the shares'. In the High Court, Lawrence J held that there was sufficient evidence for the Commissioners to come to that decision and added:

> 'I think that there was ample evidence upon which the Commissioners might come to that conclusion, and I think their conclusion is supported not only by the fact that the transactions took place at the same time, and were contained in the same documents, but also by the fact that the members of the groups were not paid with reference to the facts of the case but were paid one fixed level sum of £1,500 each, notwithstanding that some of them were performing no services and others were performing services which were valued, in the only piece of evidence there is upon the subject, at various figures.'

10.27 Not to put too fine a point on it, the compensation was therefore a mere sham and the case was deservedly lost. However, this is hardly a convincing authority on which to rely to challenge all cases of compensation. Firstly, it was not really an appeal to the High Court on a point of law, but merely whether the Commissioners had sufficient evidence to come to their decision. Secondly, the negotiations about the compensation payments had been conducted with a Mr Watts, a representative of the prospective purchasers of the shares, rather than the company itself; this fact clearly tainted the transaction in the eyes of Lawrence J:

> '. . . it is clear here that Mr Watts undertook, as part of the arrangement for the purchase of the shares, that the compensation moneys for these service agreements should be paid by the Company of which he and his nominees were acquiring control. It follows, in my opinion, that the Company's payment was not wholly and exclusively laid out for the purposes of the Company's business, because it was really laid out on account of the obligation which had been undertaken by Mr Watts.'

10.28 The Special Commissioners had held that the expense incurred was 'not required in the interests of the Company, but in the interests of the purchaser of the shares'. In the case of a purchase of own shares, the company is usually both the employer and purchaser of the shares. This should not of itself mean that the decision in *Bassett* must necessarily apply, for after all, although the company is the purchaser, it does not acquire anything.

10.29 Perhaps the biggest flaw in the use of this case as a universal weapon against compensation payments is the fact that the payments had no commercial justification. Where a compensation payment could be justified if the individual were not also a shareholder, there seems to be no valid reason why that payment should not rank as an allowable deduction for corporation tax purposes on its own merits, even if that individual were also selling shares back to the company.

10.30 Further ammunition to support a claim for a deduction for a payment of compensation can be found in the decision in *CIR v Patrick Thomson Ltd.*[1] This concerned a company operating a department store which came under the control of House of Fraser Ltd. It was the policy of House of Fraser to 'hive up' the trades of newly acquired subsidiaries and then place those companies into liquidation. The managers of the stores were paid a salary with a commission related to turnover at that store. In the case of *Patrick Thomson Ltd*, its managing director had a service contract which provided for a salary plus a commission based upon profits. This was considered by House of Fraser to be an onerous one from the point of view of Thomson. Eventually the contract was terminated by mutual agreement. The individual received a payment from Thomson of £3,000 as compensation and the company was placed in liquidation the following month.

10.31 Before the Special Commissioners the Crown argued that the expenditure had been incurred in the interests of House of Fraser not in the interests of Thomson. That company ceased to trade shortly afterwards and that cessation had been intended for some time. The Commissioners, however, felt that the benefit to House of Fraser, as the successor to the trade, was merely an effect of the expenditure rather than its purpose and that the payment was made with the object of getting rid of an onerous contract and was therefore an allowable deduction. Significantly, they also found as a fact that 'the decision to liquidate the respondent company in January 1953 was not in any way connected with the cancellation of Mr Gardiner's service agreement'.

10.32 In the Court of Session it was held that there was sufficient evidence upon which the Special Commissioners could come to their conclusion. More importantly, the judgment of Lord Clyde contained the following passage:

> 'It is found as a fact that the decision to liquidate the Company in January 1953 was not in any way connected with the cancellation of Mr Gardiner's service agreement, and these two events therefore were not part of any scheme or device to secure an advantage to Mr Gardiner at the expense of the Company. Indeed it is perfectly clear that but for the subsequent liquidation it could never be suggested that the expenditure in question was not a proper deduction from profits, for there would be no ground for saying that it was not incurred for the purposes of the trade or business.
>
> How then can the subsequent liquidation affect the matter? When the service agreement was discharged and the expenditure made, liquidation was still only a possibility. The strongest way that the matter can be put for the Crown is that there was then a present intention to liquidate at time in the future. But if that is as high as they can put it then they have not in my opinion established that the expenditure was not laid out for the purposes of the trade and the Special Commissioners were well entitled to so hold.'

10.32a If this extract could be read by substituting 'purchase of own shares' for 'liquidation', it would suggest that a payment of compensation can be an allowable deduction where there is also a purchase of own shares, provided it can be established on the evidence available that there is no inter-dependence between the two transactions.

1 (1956) 37 TC 145.

10.33 Finally it is worth considering the case of *James Snook & Co Ltd v Blasdale.*[1] Here there was a sale of shares to an acquiring company and, as part of that agreement, the purchaser agreed to procure that the target company would make a payment of compensation to a shareholder/director to resign as a director. This case is usually held out as the authority for saying that a compensation payment made at the same time as a sale of shares is not an allowable deduction for the paying company. The reality of the case was that no evidence was led before the General Commissioners which would have enabled them to find that the expenditure was incurred by the company wholly and exclusively for the purposes of its trade. In the High Court, Donovan J held that on the facts presented, the Commissioners were entitled to come to that finding. In a speech which was later quoted with approval in the Court of Appeal, he made this significant statement:[2]

> 'The mere circumstance that compensation to retiring directors is paid on a change of shareholding control does not of itself involve the consequence that such compensation can never be a deductible trading expense. So much is common ground. But it is essential in such cases that the company should prove to the Commissioners' satisfaction that it considered the question of the payment wholly untrammelled by the terms of the bargain its shareholders had struck with those who were to buy the shares and came to a decision to pay solely in the interests of its trade.
>
> This may be very difficult at times, because the persons who have to take the decision are often the persons who are to get the compensation; but any difficulty in securing an independent decision by or on behalf of the Company does not do away with the necessity of securing it if a title to deduct the compensation as a trading expense is to be sought. Evidence proving such a decision is wholly lacking here; so that the Commissioners had before them evidence establishing that payment of compensation was one of the terms of the bargain for the purchase and sale of the shares and no evidence that the Company considered the matter independently and decided to pay the compensation solely to advance its own trading interests. In those circumstances the Commissioners found that the compensation was not paid wholly and exclusively for the purposes of the Company's trade. That decision is one of fact; there is evidence to support it; and therefore I cannot interfere with it.'

10.34 It is clear therefore that not all compensation payments must automatically be regarded as part of the consideration for the purchase of the shares. There will be cases, perhaps an equity investor who is to be removed from involvement with the company, where the shares are purchased at market value and his service contract is terminated, which would justify a payment of compensation. Even if it can be established that the compensation and the purchase of own shares were independent transactions and were quite 'untrammelled' each by the other, the paying company would still need to establish a right to a tax deduction.

10.35 The distinction needs to be drawn between a payment intended as, or expressed to be, compensation for the premature termination of a service contract and an ex gratia payment to which the recipient has no legal or even

1 (1952) 33 TC 244.
2 (1952) 33 TC at p 251

moral right. It is most unlikely that a private company owned and managed by members of the same family would have service agreements and therefore any payments made to them would be ex gratia.

10.36 Perhaps the biggest hurdle to the company's entitlement to a deduction for the payment exists where the directors are all members of the same family and where the departing shareholder/director is perhaps the founder of the company. For the deduction to be successful, the company would have to show that the expenditure was 'wholly and exclusively for the purposes of the trade'. What particular benefit to the trade was intended by making this payment? In most cases involving third parties it might be argued that the payment is to induce the recipient not to do or say anything which would damage the company's reputation (this is dangerously close to being a restrictive covenant). Would the founder of a company really do anything to damage the reputation of the company he had built? Just because the purchase of the shares might be accepted as being for the benefit of the trade for the purposes of allowing capital treatment, there is no automatic reason why a payment of compensation should thereby be expended for the purposes of the trade.

Pension contributions

10.37 Despite the Revenue's attitude to 'golden handshakes', they are quite happy to see a payment into an approved pension fund for the benefit of the outgoing shareholder/director, provided such payments are within the rules of the scheme.

USES OF OWN SHARE PURCHASES

Extraction of cash

10.38 The obvious advantage of a company's power to purchase its own shares is that it brings into existence another potential purchaser for shares and one, moreover, likely to have greater financial resources than an individual. It therefore fulfils a role in being a means of extracting cash from the company either with or without a retirement.

10.39 But if a purchase is being used simply to extract cash without any withdrawal from the company, the distribution treatment will apply. Therefore why not just pay a dividend instead? The income tax and corporation tax implications will be the same. An added advantage of a dividend is that there will be no stamp duty liability. It does, however, mean paying a dividend on all the issued shares unless the other shareholders could be persuaded to waive their entitlement, but as those same shareholders would have to pass the special resolution to authorise the purchase, is that really going to be a problem?

10.40 It is only in recent years that tax advisers have really become comfortable with the idea of paying dividends. Those who remember the days of close company apportionment,[1] 'shortfall' and the like, might still be hesitant at paying dividends for fear of creating a precedent in case such concepts were re-introduced. They may also be concerned about the effect of a purchase on share values in the future. For the reasons mentioned at paragraph **10.14** above, it is not felt that an isolated purchase of own shares would have any more effect than an isolated dividend.

Creating capital losses

10.41 In the right circumstances, a purchase of own shares can be used to extract cash and create a capital loss at the same time. This will, of course only be feasible where the vendor has a high base cost for capital gains purposes, and, in the Revenue's view, is not a company. Thus it will only be a possibility where the shares were purchased from the previous holders, were held at 31 March 1982 when they had a high market value or were acquired by inheritance or gift and, in the latter case, no capital gains hold-over claim was made. Because the purchased shares are cancelled and the remaining shareholders percentage holdings are increased, this course of action is only to be recommended where the entire shareholdings are held by one shareholder or, perhaps, by a married couple. Otherwise it would be necessary for all the shareholders to sell shares in order to keep their holdings in the same ratios.

Example

Bardolph Ltd has an issued share capital of 100,000 £1 ordinary shares which are all held by Llewelyn who purchased them from the previous owners in 1993 for £500,000. The company has substantial retained profits. Llewelyn is about to sell an investment property which will give rise to a large gain.

He therefore sells 25,000 shares to the company for £250,000, which can be taken to be market value. He continues, as before, to be actively involved in the management of the company's business and therefore the purchase cannot be for the benefit of the trade. Distribution treatment will apply. Assuming there have been no previous bonus issues, the distribution will be the excess of the proceeds over the nominal value of the shares sold, £225,000. Llewelyn will pay higher rate tax of £56,250 on the combined distribution and tax credit, whilst the company will pay the same amount as advance corporation tax.

For capital gains tax purposes, the computation will be:

1 In simple terms, because of high marginal rates of income tax (at times 83%), there was an attraction in retaining profits within the company. Legislation countered this by calculating a certain level of dividends which would be expected. Where the actual dividends fell below this level, the shareholders and the company were taxed as if the shortfall had been paid out as dividends. A defence against assessment was to argue that funds needed to be retained in the company for future business needs.

	£
Proceeds	250,000
less distribution	225,000
	25,000
less cost 500,000 x 1/4	125,000
Capital loss	(100,000)

Llewelyn will therefore receive £250,000 in cash, pay £56,250 higher rate tax and generate a capital loss of £100,000 which will save him £40,000 in capital gains tax.

10.43 Could such a transaction be challenged? For the principle in *Furniss v Dawson* to apply there needs to be a series of pre-ordained transactions and steps inserted which have no commercial purpose apart from tax avoidance. Arguably there is only one transaction, the purchase of the shares, so there cannot be a 'series'. The only other transaction is the sale of the investment property and it might be difficult to show that this was part of a series. Even if it were, what steps have been inserted with no commercial motive and purely for tax avoidance? The purchase of the shares might be said to have no commercial motive in view of the fact that cash could have been extracted by a dividend instead. The mere fact that another transaction could have been carried out instead does not mean that the actual transaction did not have any commercial motive. The purchase enables the vendor to be provided with a fund of cash which he might need to pay any capital gains tax on the property sale after relief for the losses. It is therefore not immediately apparent that the Revenue could successfully apply the *Furniss v Dawson* principle.

Chapter Eleven

Redeemable Shares, New Issues

REDEEMABLE SHARES

11.1 In addition to being able to purchase their own ordinary shares, companies are also entitled to issue and subsequently redeem shares of any class. From a taxation point of view there is generally no particular difference in the tax treatment of a redemption and that of a purchase. However as indicated in Chapter Six there is, under the Revenue's current view, a specific advantage where corporate shareholders are concerned in using redeemable shares rather than irredeemable ones.

Articles of Association

11.2 A company is able to issue shares which are to be redeemed or are liable to be redeemed at the option of either the member or the company,[1] but only if empowered to do so by its articles. The articles must also contain the provisions to determine the amount of the redemption payment and the manner in which the redemption is to be made.[2]

11.3 The ability to issue redeemable shares of any class has only been available since the passing of the Companies Act 1981. Prior to that time only redeemable preference shares were permitted. Table A CA 1948, Sch 1 was not amended until 1 July 1985; therefore companies incorporated prior to that date will need to amend their articles of association to have power both to issue redeemable shares, other than preference shares, and to make provision for the manner and terms of such redemption.

11.4 Companies incorporated since 1 July 1985 which have adopted Table A will automatically have the following powers in their articles:

> 'Subject to the provisions of the Act, shares may be issued which are to be redeemed at the option of the company or the holder on such terms and in such manner as may be provided by the articles.'[3]

---

1 CA 1985 s 159(1).
2 CA 1985 s 160(3).
3 The Companies (Tables A to F) Regulations 1985 SI 1985 No 805 Table A Reg 3.

11.5 As mentioned in paragraph **2.6** private companies will also have the power to redeem those shares by means of a payment out of capital.[1]

Specific conditions

11.6 There are certain over-riding conditions which must be satisfied:

1 no redeemable shares can be issued unless at that time there is in issue at least one irredeemable share;[2]

2 (a) the shares being redeemed must be fully paid; and
  (b) the terms of redemption must provide for payment in full on redemption.[3]

Financing the redemption

11.7 As with a purchase of shares, the private company must account for the purchase in one of three ways:

1 as a payment out of distributable profits;
2 out of the proceeds of a fresh issue of shares made specifically for the purpose;[4] or,
3 as a payment out of capital.[5]

11.8 The procedures which are required are dependent on how the redemption is being funded and follow those for a purchase in the same circumstances as set out in Chapter Two.

11.9 Where the redemption is being made at a premium, however, that premium must be paid out of distributable profits only.[6] However, where the shares were originally issued at a premium, any premium on redemption may be paid out of the proceeds of a fresh issue of shares made specifically for the purposes of the redemption, up to the lower of:

1 the total of all the premiums received by the company when the shares being redeemed were originally issued; and
2 the amount of the company's share premium account including any premiums received on the issue of the new shares.

The share premium account is then to be reduced by the total premium on redemption.[7]

1 The Companies (Tables A to F) Regulations 1985 SI 1985 No 805 Table A Reg 35.
2 CA 1985 s 159(2).
3 CA 1985 s 159(3).
4 CA 1985 s 160(1)(a).
5 CA 1985 s 171(1).
6 CA 1985 s 160(1)(b).
7 A 1985 s 160(2).

Consequences of redemption

11.10 Redeemed shares are to be treated as cancelled on redemption and the company's issued share capital is reduced by their nominal value.[1] The consequences described in Chapter Two in respect of a purchase of shares also apply to a redemption.

Reporting and disclosure requirements

11.11 Within one month of the redemption the company must make a return to the Registrar of Companies on Form 122 giving details of the redemption.[2] Failure to lodge the return will render the company and every officer who is in default liable to a fine of £1,000 and a daily default fine of £100 for continued contravention.[3] In contrast to the return on Form 169 required in the case of a purchase of shares, Form 122 does not attract a liability to stamp duty.

11.12 Where a company has redeemable shares in issue, it is required to state, as part of the notes to the accounts which supplement information on the balance sheet:

1 the earliest and latest dates on which the company has the power to redeem the shares;
2 whether the shares are obliged to be redeemed or whether they are redeemable at the option of the company or the holder(s); and
3 whether a premium is payable on redemption and if so what amount.[4]

11.13 Arguably the provisions which require disclosure in the director's report in the case of a purchase of shares do not apply in the case of a redemption as that requirement covers:

1 purchases of shares; and
2 acquisitions of shares;
   (a) by forfeiture;
   (b) by surrender in lieu of forfeiture; or
   (c) 'otherwise than for valuable consideration'[5]

That aside, a redemption may be of such significance as to warrant disclosure in the director's report as an 'important event affecting the company'[6]

1 CA 1985 s 160(4).
2 CA 1985 s 122(1)(e).
3 CA 1985 s 122(2).
4 CA 1985 Sch 4 para 38(2).
5 CA 1985 Sch 7 para 7(a).
6 CA 1985 Sch 7 para 6(a).

Using redeemable shares

11.14 Given the difference in the Revenue's treatment of corporate vendors where shares are redeemed rather than purchased,[1] there is a clear advantage if shares issued within a private group were redeemable from the outset. That advantage lies in the fact that where distribution treatment applies, the amounts treated as a distribution will then be excluded from the capital gains consideration and an allowable loss may result.

11.15 That being the case, there is no tax reason why subsidiaries of private companies should not be set up with a small number of irredeemable ordinary shares and a larger number of redeemable ordinary shares which would rank *pari passu* with the irredeemable shares. Whilst, at first sight, bankers and creditors of the subsidiary may feel their position is to be weakened by the existence of the redeemable shares, the reality is that they are in no worse a position than if the entire share capital were irredeemable.

11.16 Ideally, in order to take advantage of the Revenue's publicised, if misguided, stance on corporate vendors, subsidiaries in groups of private companies should be issuing shares which are redeemable not at par, but at a premium. This premium should be determined by reference to a provision in the company's articles. This may be a value placed upon the shares by the company's auditors acting as experts.

11.17 In CA 1989 however, provisions were introduced[2] for the repeal, at a date to be appointed, of the current statutory power of redemption[3] and its replacement by new conditions. These provisions, which have not yet come into force (and it seems are unlikely to do so) would require the date of redemption to be fixed before the time the shares are issued and that the amount of the redemption consideration be fixed by the articles. It will not be possible for this amount to be the subject of any person's discretion or opinion.

Conversion of ordinary shares

11.18 The use of redeemable shares has not been common and irredeemable ordinary shares will be the norm. Thoughts may, however, turn to considering whether some existing ordinary shares might be converted into redeemable shares. A complete conversion of the ordinary share capital would not be possible due to the previously mentioned requirement that there must be at least one irredeemable share in issue at the time when redeemable shares are issued.[4]

1 See para 6.29.
2 CA 1989 s 133.
3 CA 1985 s 160(3).
4 See para 11.6.

11.19 Whilst a partial conversion of ordinary shares into redeemable ordinary shares would be theoretically possible,[1] this would require confirmation of the court.[2] By making the shares redeemable, the company is in effect seeking to reduce its share capital by paying off on redemption previously paid up capital. Whether the effort and expense would be justified is doubtful in the case of a private company. The procedures would involve the passing of a special resolution, and applying to the court for confirmation of the proposed reduction. The court will seek to protect the company's creditors by requiring the company to make provision for the amounts due to them or otherwise seeking the creditors' agreement to the reduction.[3]

11.20 Assuming that the company were prepared to go to such lengths to convert the shares, the capital gains tax consequences would need to be considered. The conversion would be treated as a reorganisation of the company's share capital, which is defined as including, inter alia, any case where there is more than one class of share and the rights attaching to any class of share are altered.[4] Such a reorganisation does not give rise to a disposal for capital gains tax purposes[5] unless the shareholder receives or is deemed to receive any consideration other than the new holding.[6] This is a logical treatment because after all, the redeemable shares would be the same shares but with different rights.

11.21 In an attempt to bring redeemable shares into existence, companies should not issue such shares as bonus shares. The value of the bonus shares would immediately give rise to a distribution by the issuing company. An advance corporation tax liability would arise on the issuing company even though the shares may have been issued to its parent company and a valid group dividend election may be in force. Such an election only allows dividends to be paid without having to account for advance corporation tax; it does not cover distributions.[7]

11.22 Where such redeemable bonus shares have been issued, and they are subsequently redeemed, a distribution will only arise on any premium payable over and above the nominal value of the shares. That part of the redemption payment equal to the nominal value, which has been charged as a distribution on issue, now represents a repayment of share capital. The amount of the distribution is the redemption payment less any amounts representing repayment of share capital.[8]

---

1 By amending the articles to change the rights attaching to those shares.
2 CA 1985 s 135(1). For companies registered in England and Wales application is to the High Court, whilst for companies registered in Scotland application is to the Court of Session, CA 1985 s 744; Insolvency Act 1986 ss 117(1) and 120(1).
3 CA 1985 ss 136 to 141.
4 TCGA 1992 s 126(2)(b).
5 TCGA 1992 s 127.
6 TCGA 1992 s 128(3).
7 TA 1988 s 247(1).
8 TA 1988 s 209(2)(b).

ISSUING NEW SHARES

Authorised share capital

11.23 In a situation where it is proposed to finance the purchase or redemption of its own shares by the proceeds of a fresh issue of shares, a company is temporarily allowed to have more shares in issue than its authorised share capital. In other words, where it is 'about' to redeem or purchase its own shares, it may issue new shares up to the nominal value of the shares to be redeemed or purchased as if those latter shares had never been issued.[1] This avoids the need to have to increase the authorised share capital in cases where there is no unissued capital.

Authority for allotment of shares

11.24 Before the directors are able to make an allotment of new shares, they must have authority to do so either in the company's articles or by an ordinary resolution of the members either in general meeting or by means of the written resolution procedure.[2] In the normal course of events, such an authority must be for a specific period of not more than five years and is capable of renewal for further periods.[3] A private company, however, can pass an elective resolution to enable the authority to be given for an indefinite period or a fixed period ending on a stated date.[4] In the context of an allotment to facilitate a purchase or redemption of own shares it is unlikely that an indefinite authority is really needed and therefore this aspect will not be considered further.

11.25 An authority which is contained in the company's articles of association will thus be limited to five years from the date those articles were adopted. In most cases this authority may have already expired and a members' resolution will be required.

11.26 The authority itself, whether in the articles or in the form of a resolution, has to state:

1 the date on which it will expire, which must not be more than five years from the company's incorporation, (where the authority is in the articles) or, otherwise, from the passing of the resolution;
2 the number of shares which may be allotted under that authority.[5]

11.27 The authority can be renewed by a resolution for a further period of up to five years. It must contain the same information as the original authority, as well as stating the number of shares still to be allotted under that

1 CA 1985 s 160(5) and as extended to purchases by s 162(2).
2 CA 1985 s 80(1).
3 CA 1985 s 80(4) and (5).
4 CA 1985 s 80A(1) and (2).
5 CA 1985 s 80(4).

original authority.[1] It is also possible to vary and revoke an authority by means of a resolution.[2]

11.28 The resolution, whether it be to grant, renew, vary or revoke the authority, is an ordinary rather than a special resolution. Thus, only a simple majority of members must vote in favour, rather than the 75% needed to vote in favour of a special resolution. Nevertheless, a copy has to be forwarded to the Registrar of Companies within 15 days of being passed.[3] This is one of the few occasions when an ordinary resolution has to be filed with the Registrar.

Pre-emption rights

11.29 Having been granted the authority to allot shares, the next step is to consider to whom the shares can be allotted. Most private companies' articles will contain provisions whereby any new shares which it is proposed to be issued must first be offered to the existing shareholders in proportion to their existing holdings. In addition, similar pre-emption rights are imposed by statute and no allotment can be made until the time allowed for acceptance of such an offer has expired or all the members have communicated their acceptance or refusal.[4] The offer must be made in writing and either made to the holder personally or sent by post.[5] The minimum period for acceptance is 21 days and the offer cannot be withdrawn within that time.[6]

11.30 A private company may, by a provision in its articles, exclude the statutory pre-emption rights and it may also make other provisions for the service of the notice of offer and the period for its acceptance.[7]

11.31 Rather than excluding the statutory pre-emption rights entirely, a company may 'disapply' those rights for a specific allotment. Thus where the directors have been given the necessary authority to allot shares, they may also be given power, either by the articles or a special resolution, to allot shares under their power ignoring the statutory pre-emption rights, in whole of in part as they think fit.[8] Alternatively they may be given a more restricted authority by a special resolution to ignore the statutory pre-emption rights in respect of a specified allotment of shares.[9]

11.32 The special resolution to disapply the statutory pre-emption rights is not to be proposed unless it is recommended by the directors. When the resolution is circulated to the members with the notice of the meeting, it should be accompanied by a written statement from the directors giving their reasons for making the recommendation, the amount to be paid to the company in

1 CA 1985 s 80(5).
2 CA 1985 s 80(4).
3 CA 1985 s 80(8).
4 CA 1985 s 89(1)(a).
5 CA 1985 s 90(2).
6 CA 1985 s 90(6).
7 CA 1985 s 91(1).
8 CA 1985 s 95(1).
9 CA 1985 s 95(2).

respect of the shares and their justification of that amount.[1] Anyone who is responsible for the circularisation of a misleading, false or deceptive statement could be liable to imprisonment or a fine or both.[2]

11.33 Even where the company has taken steps to exclude or disapply the statutory pre-emption rights, it has still to deal with any such rights which may be contained in its articles. This may require those members not taking up any new shares to formally waive their rights under the articles in respect of that allotment.

Taxation consequences

11.34 Apart from a general prohibition that the shares may not be allotted at a discount on nominal value,[3] there is no other company law requirement governing the price at which shares should be allotted. In the normal case it would be expected that the purchase of own shares would proceed at market value and therefore the new issue of shares would be at the same figure. However there may well be cases where the shares are issued at a price which is either above or below market value and the taxation consequences of each need to be considered.

Allotment below market value

11.35 The consequences depend upon the current relationship of the allottee to the company.

Current employee who is not already a shareholder

11.36 If the opportunity to subscribe for the shares arises from the individual's employment, the excess of the market value of the shares allotted over the consideration paid is charged as an emolument under the normal rules of Schedule E[4] following the decision in *Weight v Salmon*.[5] In that case a director was given the opportunity to subscribe for shares at an undervalue. It was held that the opportunity was the receipt of 'money's worth' in respect of the successful exercise of his office and as such was a 'profit' from the employment.

11.37 Even if it is possible to show that the opportunity does not arise from the employment, but from some other cause, this is unlikely to avoid an income tax liability. If the individual is a director or 'higher paid employee,' a charge will arise under the benefits legislation[6] regardless of the reason why the opportunity arises. This is because, for such individuals, all 'benefits' received are deemed to be by reason of the employment.[7]

---

1 CA 1985 s 95(5).
2 CA 1985 s 95(6).
3 CA 1985 s 100(1).
4 TA 1988 s 131(1).
5 (1934) 19 TC 174.
6 TA 1988 s 154.
7 TA 1988 s 168(3).

11.38 If the employee is a 'higher paid employee' or a director, and does not pay up the full amount of the issue price at the time of issue, he or she will be regarded as being in receipt of a notional loan from the company.[1] The loan is equal to the excess of the market value over the amount actually paid for the shares less any amount which has already been charged to tax as an emolument.[2] No tax will, however, be charged if the aggregate amount of the notional loan and any actual loans do not exceed £5,000.[3]

Example

A higher paid employee is allotted 10,000 shares at £2.50 per share when the current market value of those shares is £4.00 per share. He only pays £1.30 per share on allotment and is not charged any interest on the amount of the allotment price still outstanding. The tax position will be:

1 he or she will be assessed under the normal rules of Schedule E to emoluments of £15,000 (10,000 shares at £4.00 less £2.50);
2 he or she will then be assessed on a benefit comprising interest at the official rate on a notional loan of :

	£
'Undervalue': 10,000 shares at market value	40,000
less amount paid on allotment	13,000
	27,000
less amount charged as an emolument	15,000
	12,000

11.39 The notional loan will be reduced as and when he or she pays the balance of the allotment price[4] and will be regarded as terminated when either:

1 the allotment price has been fully paid:
2 the employee is released from any obligation to make any further payments of the allotment price;
3 the shares are no longer held by the employee or any person connected with him; or
4 the employee dies.[5]

11.40 Where either circumstance (2) or (3) applies, the amount of the notional loan outstanding at that time is treated as having been written off by the employer and a corresponding amount is assessed as a benefit.[6]

11.41 If shares are to be allotted to an employee of a company which is a subsidiary of another company, care will have to be taken to ensure that a charge does not accidentally fall to be made on the growth in value of the

1 TA 1988 s 162(1).
2 TA 1988 s 162(3).
3 TA 1988 s 161(1)(a).
4 TA 1988 s 162(3)(b).
5 TA 1988 s 162(4).
6 TA 1988 s 160(2) by virtue of TA 1988 s 162(5).

shares. This charge will arise where the issuing company is a 'dependant subsidiary'. Every subsidiary company is a 'dependent subsidiary' for an accounting period unless it satisfies the following conditions:

1 the whole or substantially the whole of its business is carried on with persons who are not members of the same group of companies;
2 the value of the company has not increased in value by more than 5% as a result of intra-group transactions;
3 within two years of the end of the accounting period the directors of the principal company in the group certify to the inspector that, in their opinion, conditions (1) and (2) have been satisfied; and
4 that directors' certificate is accompanied by a report from the auditors of the subsidiary stating that they have enquired into the affairs of the company particularly with reference to conditions (1) and (2) and are not aware of anything to indicate that the directors' opinion is unreasonable.[1]

11.42 This is a particularly invidious piece of legislation as, even if conditions (1) and (2) are clearly satisfied, the company will nevertheless be regarded as a dependent subsidiary if the directors and auditors overlook the requirement at (3) and (4).

11.43 Where the issuing company is a dependent subsidiary at the time the shares are allotted, the employee will be chargeable under Schedule E on the whole of the increase in value of the shares on the seventh anniversary of the issue or the time he or she disposes of them, if earlier.[2]

11.44 If the issuing company is not a dependent subsidiary at the time the shares are allotted, but becomes one subsequently, a charge (on the increase in value from the time when the company became a dependent subsidiary) arises on the earliest of:

1 the seventh anniversary of the company becoming a dependent subsidiary;
2 the time when he or she disposes of the shares; or
3 the time when the company ceases to be a dependent subsidiary, if it ever does so.[3]

Existing shareholder

11.45 Even if the existing shareholder is also a director or higher paid employee, their opportunity to subscribe for the new shares arises, not by reason of their employment, but from their rights as a shareholder. This is particularly the case where that opportunity arises under any pre-emption rights contained in the articles or the statutory pre-emption rights referred to earlier.[4]

1 FA 1988 s 86(1).
2 FA 1988 s 79(2).
3 FA 1988 s 79(3).
4 Para 11.29

11.46 The question which then arises is whether the 'undervalue' can be charged to tax on the shareholder as some form of distribution. Looking at the normal distribution rules,[1] there are only two possible ways in which a distribution could arise; where there has been a 'distribution out of the assets of the company'[2] and where there has been a 'transfer of assets or liabilities by a company to its members'[3] or vice versa. In the latter case, the excess of the value of the benefit received by the member over the consideration he has given is a distribution. It is difficult to see how the mere allotment of shares can constitute a distribution out of the assets of the company, as this implies a reduction of the company's assets. On the other hand, there has been a transfer of assets by the member to the company and the value he has received in the form of the shares is in excess of the consideration he has provided. Therefore there would seem to be a distribution arising in this situation.

Other shareholders

11.47 Whilst one shareholder may be benefiting from the allotment, the remaining shareholders will see their holdings reduced in value. If they have waived their pre-emption rights to allow the allotment to occur, or indeed have simply not exercised their rights, they may well have made transfers of value for inheritance tax purposes.[4] These would, however, be potentially exempt transfers so that no actual tax liability would arise, provided that none of the 'transferors' died within seven years, and, of course, subject to the availability of the nil rate band and annual exemptions. A defence against such a transfer of value would be to claim that the omission to exercise the right was not deliberate[5] or that it was not intended 'to confer any gratuitous benefit' upon the recipient shareholder.[6] In other words, the recipient shareholder was the only one able, or prepared, to subscribe to the new shares.

11.48 Another inheritance tax aspect is whether the company can be said to have made a transfer of value. In such a case the amount of the transfer is apportioned to the individual shareholders in proportion to their interests in the company.[7] A de minimis rule provides that no apportionment is to be made to anyone with an interest of 5% or less.[8] The danger here is that any transfer of value apportioned to a company participator is not to be treated as a potentially exempt transfer.[9] Therefore an immediate liability could arise, depending again upon the amounts involved and the availability of annual exemptions and the nil rate band.

1 TA 1988 s 209.
2 TA 1988 s 209(2)(b).
3 TA 1988 s 209(4).
4 IHTA 1984 s 3(3).
5 IHTA 1984 s 3(3).
6 IHTA 1984 s 10(1) – see para 10.6.
7 IHTA 1984 s 94.
8 IHTA 1984 s 94(4).
9 IHTA 1984 s 3A(6) because s 94 introduces a charge 'as if a transfer of value had been made' by the participators.

11.49 Even though the company is a trading company it is unlikely that business property relief would be available in either scenario. This relief is only available where the value transferred is 'attributable to the value of relevant business property'.[1] It is arguable that the value is actually attributable to a chose in action, the shareholder's pre-emption rights rather than the value of the shares themselves.

11.50 If there is an element of bounty in a shareholder's decision to waive pre-emption rights, the income tax settlement provisions may be in point. Where the recipient of the shares issued at an undervalue is the minor child of another shareholder, any dividends paid subsequently on those shares could be assessed on the parent.[2] The same consequence would result if the recipients of the shares were the trustees of a settlement in which another shareholder was the settlor and also had an interest as a beneficiary or potential beneficiary.

Allotment above market value

11.51 As the allottee will, in such a situation be receiving shares worth less than his subscription, the only question is whether by doing so there is a transfer of value for inheritance tax purposes. If so, the transfer will be a potentially exempt transfer and no liability will arise if the shareholder survives for seven years from the date of the allotment.

1 IHTA 1984 s 104(1).
2 TA 1988 s 660B.

Chapter Twelve

CONTRACTUAL PROBLEMS

FAILURE TO COMPLETE

12.1 Should it come to pass that the company, having entered into the contract to acquire any of its own shares, or having issued redeemable shares, fails to complete the purchase or to redeem the shares, it has no liability in damages for its failure.[1] It is always open to the aggrieved shareholder to apply to the court for an order for specific performance, but the court cannot grant such an order if the company can show that it cannot meet the costs of the purchase or redemption out of its distributable profits.[2] All that appears to be left for the shareholder is to apply for an injunction preventing the company from paying dividends to other shareholders until sufficient distributable profits have been amassed to enable the purchase or redemption to proceed. The vendor, however, will still have the voting power on the shares concerned[3] and may be able to exploit his or her nuisance value by means of that power.

12.2 Where the reason for the failure to complete the purchase, or to redeem the shares, is the commencement of winding up, the terms of the purchase or redemption may be enforced against the company[4] provided that the transaction should have taken place before the commencement of winding up and that the company could have made a lawful distribution equal to the purchase or redemption price.[5] However that purchase price has to rank behind amounts due to creditors and to holders of shares with superior rights to capital.[6] In effect this only gives the potential vendor a marginally better position in the pecking order than his or her fellow shareholders of the same class.

DELAYED COMPLETION

Purchases

12.3 In the normal course of events, the purchase contract, if in writing, will be signed and completion will occur on the same day. There may, however, be

1 CA 1985 s 178(1) and (2).
2 CA 1985 s 178(3).
3 See para 9.22.
4 CA 1985 s 178(4).
5 CA 1985 s 178(5).
6 CA 1985 s 178(6).

cases where a gap occurs between contract and completion either intentionally or by default. It may also be that completion never takes place.

12.4 The delay between the contract and its ultimate completion, should that ever happen, will have significant taxation consequences. For capital gains tax purposes, where the disposal is by way of a contract, the date of the disposal is the date of the unconditional contract, or in the case of a contract subject to conditions, the date that those conditions are satisfied.[1]

12.5 Where completion is intentionally delayed, the vendor may claim to pay any capital gains tax liability by instalments where the consideration for the sale is receivable by instalments over a period of 18 months or more.[2] That apart, the normal rule is that the gain is to be calculated on the full amount of the consideration due with no deduction for any risk that it may not be received. However, if it should turn out that any amount is irrecoverable, an appropriate reduction can be made in the sales proceeds used to compute the chargeable gain.[3]

12.6 In practice, the failure to complete the purchase should be known well before the vendor needs to declare the liability arising out of that transaction. It may be that a resolution of the situation can be achieved, perhaps by the parties agreeing to cancel the contract.[4] However, if the contract is still in existence, it will be up to the vendor to claim that the consideration due under the contract is irrecoverable.

12.7 Fortunately, as the purchase proceeds would not actually become payable until completion, the vendor cannot be a loan creditor in respect of those proceeds and therefore cannot by that means be regarded as connected with the company.

12.8 A purchase which attracts distribution treatment is more complex. It is clear that a distribution only occurs when a payment is made.[5] Unfortunately even under the distribution treatment there is a capital gains tax disposal and therefore once again, strictly speaking a liability arises when the contract comes into existence. Normally that part of the proceeds which forms part of the recipient's income is excluded from the consideration for capital gains tax purposes. But, as the consideration has not been received, it cannot yet be part of the vendor's income and would remain chargeable to capital gains tax. The option to pay tax by instalments, where the consideration for the disposal is itself payable by instalments,[6] is not going to be available. In such a situation the only course open may be to ask the Revenue to adopt a pragmatic approach and wait until such time as the position can be resolved. A claim can then be made that the consideration has become irrecoverable.[7]

1 TCGA 1992 s 28.
2 TCGA 1992 s 280.
3 TCGA 1992 s 48.
4 See para 12.10.
5 This seems to be implicit in the language used in s 209 TA 1988.
6 TCGA 1992 s 280.
7 TCGA 1992 s 48.

Redemptions

12.9 The tax position with regard to redemptions is different again. The terms upon which redeemable shares are to be redeemed will be contained in the company's articles of association and will usually give either the company or the shareholder the right to opt for redemption within a specified timescale. As the disposal is triggered by a notice from one side or another, it is believed that the disposal is not 'under a contract'[1] and therefore there cannot be the same hiatus between contract and completion as in the case of a purchase. The Revenue's view[2] is that a redemption creates a disposal because the receipt of a capital distribution is deemed to be a disposal of an interest in the shares.[3] Regardless of whether this view is correct, the date of disposal has to be determined under the normal capital gains rule which is the date that the consideration is received. As no consideration has been received, there can be no disposal.

VARYING OR CANCELLING THE PURCHASE CONTRACT

12.10 If, following the making of a contract for the purchase of some of its own shares, the company wishes to seek an agreement with the shareholder to be released from the contract, it can only do so if authorised by a special resolution.[4] Similarly if it wishes to vary the terms of the contract, it must also have the authority of a special resolution.[5] These resolutions are subject to the same procedural requirements as applied to the special resolution which authorised the original contract.

12.11 If, as part of that new agreement, the company makes a payment to the vendor, he or she will probably be facing a capital gains tax liability on that amount. The subject matter of the disposal would normally be the vendor's rights under the original contract, ie a chose in action, rather than the shares which were the subject of that contract. That is the Revenue's view of the strict position as set out in Concession D33. This concession was issued after it was held that the right to take action for compensation or damages is an asset for capital gains tax purposes.[6]

12.12 It is perhaps debatable whether a vendor in this position has a right of action, when company law says that, because of the over-riding need to protect creditors, he or she cannot sue the company for damages. In the final analysis however, the vendor has received a capital sum in respect of an asset. It is either in respect of the shares themselves, or more likely, the rights under

1 TCGA 1992 s 28.
2 Inland Revenue Capital Gains Manual CG 58655.
3 TCGA 1992 s 122.
4 CA 1985 s 167(2).
5 CA 1985 s 164(7).
6 *Zim Properties Ltd v Proctor* (1984) 58 TC 371.

the original contract. If the latter then Concession D33 should apply and treat the gain as arising on the underlying asset, ie the shares. This must follow from the wording of paragraph 1 of the concession; '. . . a person who receives compensation or damages, whether by court order, arbitration *or by negotiated settlement* as a result of a cause of action may be regarded as disposing of the right of action' (emphasis added). Whilst the vendor cannot sue for damages, he or she still has a right of action to apply for an order for specific performance or an injunction as mentioned earlier.[1] Therefore the subject matter of the disposal will always be the underlying shares and retirement relief, if appropriate, will still be available.

12.13 A highly contentious method of avoiding the distribution treatment therefore suggests itself. After having entered into a contract to purchase shares which would have attracted the distribution treatment, the company might make a payment, probably much smaller than the proposed purchase price, to be released from the contract. The payment should be liable to capital gains tax in the hands of the recipient. The Revenue would probably refuse to apply Concession D33 and would be justified in so doing.[2] The individual would be treated as disposing of a chose in action which would have no base cost, rather than the shares which should have some cost attaching to them. However the company would not have a liability to advance corporation tax.

12.14 As the prospective vendor would still have his or her shareholding, it would be difficult to quantify any loss that he or she might have suffered by the cancellation. There may have been a 'lost opportunity' cost in not having the cash proceeds available to make other investments. Prima facie the Revenue could claim that a distribution arose as a benefit had been provided to a participator.[3]

INVALID PURCHASES

12.15 Where the particular requirements of company law have not been fully observed, then apart from the various fines and penalties mentioned at paragraph **2.53** which may be applicable, the purchase or redemption will be invalid. Of course, payment for the shares may have already have been made before a purchase or redemption is subsequently discovered to be invalid. In these circumstances the vendor will hold the sales proceeds as a constructive trustee for the company and can therefore be called upon to repay those funds.

12.16 From a taxation point of view, an invalid purchase or redemption does not constitute a disposal of the shares, nor a distribution. It would be

1 See para 12.1.
2 *R v Inspector of Taxes, Reading ex p Fulford-Dobson* [1987] STC 344, 60 TC 168.
3 ICTA 1988 s 418.

the making of a loan to a participator which, assuming the company was 'close',[1] would give rise to a tax liability on the company equal to the advance corporation tax payable on a distribution of the same amount.[2] There would also be a deemed distribution in respect of the benefit of the loan,[3] measured in the same way as the benefit on an interest free loan to a director.[4] Thus the shareholder would have a potential liability to higher rate tax and the company a liability to advance corporation tax on the amount of that benefit.

1 TA 1988 s 414.
2 TA 1988 s 419.
3 TA 1988 s 418(2).
4 TA 1988 s 418(4).

Appendix One

PRECEDENTS, FORMS, AND STATEMENTS OF PRACTICE

The precedents in this Appendix are intended to be illustrative rather than definitive. Amendments will be required to adapt them to the circumstances of any particular case.

1 FORM OF CONSENT FOR SHORT NOTICE FOR EXTRAORDINARY GENERAL MEETING.[1]

[ ] Limited

('the Company')

Companies Act 1985 Section 369(3)

We the undersigned, being members of the above-named Company having the right to attend and vote at the Extraordinary General Meeting of the Company to be held on [ ] ('the Meeting') and together holding not less than 95[2] per cent in nominal value of the shares giving that right hereby agree to accept shorter notice of that meeting than that specified in Companies Act 1985 Section 369(2) or in the Company's Articles of Association.

____________________ Date ____________________

____________________ Date ____________________

1 Where the necessary special resolution(s) are to be passed at a meeting of the members, CA 1985 s 369(2) and regulation 38 of Table A require members to be given 21 days clear notice of the meeting. This can be avoided by the consent of members holding not less than 95% of the nominal issued share capital, see para **2.15**.

2 This consent can be given by the holders of 90% of the voting power if an elective resolution to this effect has previously been passed, see para **2.15**.

2 NOTICE OF EXTRAORDINARY GENERAL MEETING[1]

[ ] Limited

('the Company')

NOTICE IS HEREBY GIVEN that an Extraordinary General Meeting of the Company will be held at [ ] on [ ] for the purpose of considering and, if thought fit, passing the following special resolutions,[2] namely:

[INSERT APPROPRIATE RESOLUTIONS]

By Order of the Board

________________________ Date ________________________

[Registered Office]

Note: A member entitled to attend and vote at the above Extraordinary General Meeting may appoint a proxy to attend and, on a poll, vote in his stead. A proxy need not be a member of the Company.

1 Even though the shareholders may have consented to accept less than 21 days' notice of the EGM, there is still a need to issue a notice calling the meeting.

2 If there are both special and ordinary resolutions being proposed, amend the wording to 'the following resolutions, of which No x will be proposed as an ordinary resolution and No x will be proposed as a special resolution.'

3 FORM OF WRITTEN RESOLUTION[1]

Company No [ ]

[ ] LIMITED

('the Company')

WRITTEN RESOLUTION[2]

PURSUANT TO COMPANIES ACT 1985 SECTION 381A

In accordance with Companies Act 1985 section 381A we, the undersigned, being all[3] the members of the company entitled at the date hereof to attend and vote at general meetings of the Company HEREBY AGREE AND CONFIRM that the following resolution shall for all purposes have effect as if it had been passed by the Company in general meeting. Accordingly we HEREBY RESOLVE:

[INSERT APPROPRIATE RESOLUTIONS]

____________________________ Date ________________________

1 Where there is unanimous agreement of the shareholders, a shareholders' meeting need not take place and all formalities can be dealt with by means of the written resolution procedures, see paragraph **2.20**.

2 It is not necessary that all members should sign the same document. In fact it is probably more convenient to send a separate but identical document to each member for signature (except, of course, the vendor).

3 In the case of a resolution to approve the purchase or redemption, the vendor shareholder is specifically excluded from being regarded as a member who would be entitled to attend and vote and his or her signature is not required for the resolution to be valid (in fact it would make the resolution invalid, see para **2.17**). However the vendor's signature will be required for any other written resolutions to be valid and therefore he or she should sign a document containing only those other resolutions.

4 RESOLUTION TO APPROVE A PURCHASE OF OWN SHARES[1]

THAT the terms of the contract[2] (a copy of which is at the Company's registered office and a copy of which has been sent to all members of the Company on or before the date of this resolution) for the purchase by the Company from the shareholder named in the said contract of a total of [ ] Ordinary Shares of [ ] each in the capital of the Company be and are hereby approved and that the directors be authorised to enter into the said contract on behalf of the Company.

[N.B. If the payment is to be wholly or partly out of capital then the following additional resolution is required.]

2. THAT a payment of £[ ] out of the capital of the company, as defined in Companies Act 1985 sections 171 and 172 and as specified in the statutory declaration made by the directors on [ ] (a copy of which, together with a copy of the auditor's report, is at the Company's registered office and has been sent to all members of the Company on or before the date of this resolution) in respect of the purchase of the above mentioned shares be and is hereby authorised and approved.

---

1 If these resolutions are to be passed as written resolutions each member, other than the vendor, should be sent a copy of the contract (or a memorandum of its terms) with the written resolution (and a copy if the director's statutory declaration and auditor's report if appropriate), see para **2.20**.

2 If it is not proposed to have a written contract then a written memorandum of the terms of the purchase has to be circulated and the wording of the resolution will need appropriate amendment.

5 RESOLUTION TO AMEND ARTICLES TO EMPOWER COMPANY TO PURCHASE ITS OWN SHARES[1]

THAT the following regulation be and is hereby incorporated into the company's articles of association as regulation number [ ];

'Subject to the provisions of the Companies Act 1985, the Company may purchase its own shares (including any redeemable shares) and, if it is a private company, make a payment in respect of the redemption or purchase of its own shares otherwise than out of distributable profits of the company or the proceeds of a fresh issue of shares.'

1 This will only be required if the company does not already have the power in its articles via the adoption of the current version of Table A. Where, however, the company was of such antiquity that its articles were originally drafted to comply with earlier Companies Acts (eg 1929 or earlier) it would probably be prudent to take the opportunity to adopt an entirely new set of articles.

6 RESOLUTIONS TO ISSUE NEW SHARES

1. THAT the Board be and are hereby given unconditional authority for the purposes of section 80 Companies Act 1985 ('the Act') to allot relevant securities up to a maximum nominal amount of [£] provided that this authority shall expire five years[1] from the date of the passing of this resolution.[2]

2. THAT, as permitted by section 96 of the Act, the directors be and are hereby authorised to allot the shares referred to in resolution 1 above as if the pre-emption rights contained in section 89(1) of the Act did not apply to such allotments.[3]

---

1 This is the maximum permissible period for which authority can be given, unless the company has passed an elective resolution providing for a longer or even an indefinite period, see para **11.24**. In most cases where the shares are being issued to fund the purchase of own shares a period of 12 months would be more than adequate.

2 This is an ordinary resolution and as such only requires a simple majority of the votes cast if passed at a shareholders' meeting.

3 This, by contrast, is a special resolution and therefore requires 75% of the votes cast if passed at a shareholders' meeting.

7 RESOLUTION TO AMEND ARTICLES TO ENABLE THE ISSUE OF REDEEMABLE SHARES[1]

THAT the following regulation be and is hereby incorporated into the company's articles of association as regulation number [ ];

Subject to the provisions of the Companies Act 1985, shares may be issued which are to be redeemed at the option of the Company or the holder on such terms and in such manner as may be provided by these articles.

1 This will only be required if the company does not already have the power in its articles via the adoption of the current version of Table A.

8 MINUTES OF EXTRAORDINARY GENERAL MEETING

[ ] Limited

('the Company')

MINUTES of an Extraordinary General Meeting of the Company held at [ ] on [ ] at [ ]am/pm

PRESENT: (Chairman)

IN ATTENDANCE:

The Chairman reported that, as a quorum was present and that the necessary majority of the members had consented to holding the meeting at short notice, [he/she] declared the meeting open.

With the consent of all the members present the Notice convening the meeting was taken as read.

The Chairman proposed and [ ] seconded, resolution No 1 as a [special/ordinary] resolution which was passed by the necessary majority.

[REPEAT AS NECESSARY FOR ANY OTHER RESOLUTIONS]

There being no further business the Chairman declared the meeting closed.

____

Chairman

9 FORM OF RESOLUTIONS FOR SUBMISSION TO REGISTRAR OF COMPANIES

Company No [ ]

[ ] LIMITED

('the Company')

RESOLUTION(S)

Passed on [ ]

At an Extraordinary General Meeting of the Company, held on [ ], the following resolution(s) were passed as [special/ordinary] resolutions;

[INSERT THE APPROPRIATE RESOLUTIONS]

____

Chairman

10 SHARE PURCHASE CONTRACT

THIS PURCHASE CONTRACT is made the [ ] day of [ ] 199[ ]

BETWEEN

1. [ ] LIMITED a company incorporated in [ ] (Registered Number [ ]) and having its registered office at [ ] ('the Company')

and

2. [ ] of [ ] ('the Shareholder')

WHEREAS

1. The authorised share capital of the Company at the date hereof consists of £[ ] divided into [ ] Ordinary Shares of [ ] each of which [ ] have been issued and are or are credited as being fully paid up.

2. The Shareholder is the registered holder and beneficial owner of [ ] Ordinary shares in the capital of the Company of which the Company has agreed to purchase [ ] Ordinary Shares ('the Sale Shares')

3. The Company is authorised by its Articles of Association to purchase its own shares.

4. The terms of this Contract have been authorised by a [written/special] resolution of the Company pursuant to section 381A of the Companies Act 1985 duly passed on [ ]

NOW THEREFORE IT IS HEREBY AGREED as follows:

1. The Shareholder shall sell to the Company as beneficial owner and the Company shall purchase the Sale Shares free from all liens charges and encumbrances for the sum of £[ ].

2. Completion of the purchase of the Sale Shares shall be constituted by:

   (a) the Shareholder surrendering to the Company the share certificates relative to the Sale Shares; and
   (b) the Company delivering a banker's draft for the purchase price to the Shareholder

3. This Contract shall in all respects be governed by and construed in accordance with the law of [ ]

AS WITNESS the hands of the duly authorised representative of the Company and the Shareholder the day and year first before written

11 DIRECTORS' STATUTORY DECLARATION OF SOLVENCY (FORM 173)

2.63

G

COMPANIES FORM No.173

Declaration in relation to the redemption or purchase of shares out of capital

173

Please do not write in this margin

Pursuant to section 173 of the Companies Act 1985

Please complete legibly, preferably in black type, or bold block lettering

To the Registrar of Companies
(Address overleaf - Note 4)

For official use

Company number

Name of company

* insert full name of company

*

Note
Please read the notes on page 2 before completing this form.

ø insert name(s) and address(es) of all the directors

I/We ø

† delete as appropriate

[the sole director][all the directors]† of the above company do solemnly and sincerely declare that:

§ delete whichever is inappropriate

The business of the company is:

(a) that of a [recognised bank][licensed institution]† within the meaning of the Banking Act 1979§

(b) that of a person authorised under section 3 or 4 of the Insurance Companies Act 1982 to carry on insurance business in the United Kingdom§

(c) that of something other than the above§

The company is proposing to make a payment out of capital for the redemption or purchase of its own shares

The amount of the permissible capital payment for the shares in question is £
(note 1)

Continued overleaf

Presentor's name address and reference (if any):

For official Use

General Section	Post room

Page 1

I/We have made full enquiry into the affairs and prospects of the company, and I/we have formed the opinion:

Please do not write in this margin

Please complete legibly, preferably in black type, or bold block lettering

(a) as regards its initial situation immediately following the date on which the payment out of capital is proposed to be made, that there will be no grounds on which the company could then be found unable to pay its deuts (note 2), and

(b) as regards its prospects for the year immediately following that date, that, having regard to my/our intentions with respect to the management of the company's business during that year and to the amount and character of the financial resources which will in my/our view be available during that year, the company will be able to continue to carry on business as a going concern (and will accordingly be able to pay its debts as they fall due) throughout that year.(note 2)

And I/we make this solemn declaration conscientiously believing the same to be true and by virtue of the provisions of the Statutory Declarations Act 1835.

Declared at ______________________________

____

____

the ________ day of ______________________

one thousand nine hundred and ______________

____

before me ______________________________

A Commissioner for Oaths, or Notary Public, or Justice of the Peace, or Solicitor having the powers conferred on a Commissioner for Oaths.

Declarant(s) to sign below

Notes

1 'Permissible capital payment' means an amount which, taken together with
(i) any available profits of the company; and
(ii) the proceeds of any fresh issue of shares made for the purposes of the redemption or purchase;
is equal to the price of redemption or purchase.
'Available profits' means the company's profits which are available for distribution (within the meaning of section 172 and 263 of the Companies Act 1985).
The question whether the company has any profits so available and the amount of any such profits is to be determined in accordance with section 172 of the Companies Act 1985.

2 Contingent and prospective liabilities of the company must be taken into account, see sections 173(4) & 517 of the Companies Act 1985.

3 A copy of this declaration together with a copy of the auditors report required by section 173 of the Companies Act 1985, must be delivered to the Registrar of Companies not later than the day on which the company publishes the notice required by section 175(1) of the Companies Act 1985, or first publishes or gives the notice required by section 175(2), whichever is the earlier.

4 The address for companies registered in England and Wales or Wales is:-

The Registrar of Companies
Companies House
Crown Way
Cardiff
CF4 3UZ

or, for companies registered in Scotland:-

The Registrar of Companies
Companies House
100-102 George Street
Edinburgh
EH2 3DJ

Page 2

12 AUDITORS' REPORT UNDER COMPANIES ACT 1985 s 173(5)

The Directors

[ ] Ltd

Dear Sirs,

Companies Act 1985 section 173

We refer to your statutory declaration under Companies Act 1985, section 173(3) in respect of the proposed payment of £[ ] for the purchase of [ ] of the Company's own shares.

We have inquired into the company's state of affairs and the amount specified in the declaration as the permissible capital payment is, in our view, properly determined in accordance with Companies Act 1985, sections 171 and 172. We are not aware of anything to indicate that the opinion expressed by you in the declaration is unreasonable in all the circumstances.

Yours faithfully,

13 NOTICE TO BE INSERTED IN THE GAZETTE AND A NATIONAL NEWSPAPER.

[ ] Limited

Company number [ ]

Notice is hereby given that:

A [unanimous written/special] resolution was passed on [ ] to authorise the payment of £[ ] out of the capital of the company in connection with the purchase of certain of the company's own shares . The permissible capital payment was £[ ].

The relevant statutory declaration and auditor's report are available for inspection at the company's registered office, [ ].

Within five weeks immediately following the date of the above mentioned written resolution, any creditor of the company may apply to the High Court under Companies Act 1985 section 176 for an order prohibiting the payment.

14 RETURN TO COMPANIES HOUSE (FORM 169)

G

COMPANIES FORM No. 169

Return by a company purchasing its own shares

2.62

169

Pursuant to section 169 of the Companies Act 1985

Please do not write in this margin

Please complete legibly, preferably in black type, or bold block lettering

To the Registrar of Companies
(Address overleaf)

For official use

Company number

Please do not write in the space below. For Inland Revenue use only.

Name of company

* insert full name of company

*

Note
This return must be delivered to the Registrar within a period of 28 days beginning with the first date on which shares to which it relates were delivered to the company

Shares were purchased by the company under section 162 of the above Act as follows:

Class of shares			
Number of shares purchased			
Nominal value of each share			
Date(s) on which the shares were delivered to the company			
Maximum prices paid § for each share			
Minimum prices paid § for each share			

§ A private company is not required to give this information

The aggregate amount paid by the company for the shares to which this return relates was:	£
Stamp duty payable pursuant to section 66 of the Finance Act 1986 on the aggregate amount at 50p per £100 or part of £100	£

‡ Insert Director, Secretary, Receiver, Administrator, Administrative Receiver or Receiver (Scotland) as appropriate

Signed　　Designation‡　　Date

Presentor's name address and reference (if any):

For official Use
General Section　　Post room

15 RETURN OF REDEMPTIONS TO COMPANIES HOUSE (FORM 122)

2.23

G

COMPANIES FORM No. 122

Notice of consolidation, division, sub-division, redemption or cancellation of shares, or conversion, re-conversion of stock into shares

122

Please do not write in this margin

Pursuant to section 122 of the Companies Act 1985

Please complete legibly, preferably in black type, or bold block lettering

To the Registrar of Companies
(Address overleaf)

For official use

Company number

Name of company

* insert full name of company

*

gives notice that:

‡ Insert Director, Secretary, Administrator, Administrative Receiver or Receiver (Scotland) as appropriate

Signed

Designation‡

Date

Presentor's name address and reference (if any):

For official Use
General Section
Post room

16 NOTICE TO THE INSPECTOR OF TAXES UNDER TA 1988 s 226

H M Inspector of Taxes

[ ]District

Dear Sir,

[ ]Ltd, Reference:[ ]

In accordance with TA 1988 s 226(1) we hereby give you notice on behalf of our above named client that it made a payment on [ ] to which s 219 applies. The transaction has been carried out precisely in accordance with the clearance granted by Company Tax Division on [ ] under reference [ ].

Yours faithfully

17 STATEMENT OF PRACTICE SP2/82 (CURRENT VERSION)

Where a company makes a purchase of own shares which involves a payment in excess of the capital originally subscribed for the shares, the excess constitutes a distribution. However, such a payment is treated as not giving rise to a distribution if, among other conditions, the purchase is made wholly or mainly to benefit a trade carried on by the company, or by one of its 75 per cent subsidiaries. This Statement indicates how this test is applied by the Revenue.

The Annex to this Statement gives guidance on how companies should apply for a ruling on whether or not a purchase will be treated as a distribution.

The 'trade benefit test' TA 1988 s 219(1)(a)

1 The company's sole or main purpose in making the payment must be to benefit a trade carried on by it or by its 75 per cent subsidiary. The condition is not satisfied where, for example, the transaction is designed to serve the personal or wider commercial interests of the vending shareholder (although usually he will benefit from it) or where the intended benefit for the company is to some non-trading activity which it also carries on.

2 If there is disagreement between the shareholders over the management of the company and that disagreement is having or is expected to have an adverse effect on the company's trade, then the purchase will be regarded as satisfying the trade benefit test provided the effect of the transaction is to remove the dissenting shareholder entirely. Similarly, if the purpose is to ensure that an unwilling shareholder who wishes to end his association with the company does not sell his shares to someone who might not be acceptable to the other shareholders, the purchase will normally be regarded as benefiting the company's trade.

Examples of unwilling shareholders are:

(a) an outside shareholder who has provided equity finance (whether or not with the expectation of redemption or sale to the company) and who now wishes to withdraw that finance;
(b) a controlling shareholder who is retiring as a director and wishes to make way for new management;
(c) personal representatives of a deceased shareholder, where they wish to realise the value of the shares;
(d) a legatee of a deceased shareholder, where he does not wish to hold shares in the company.

3 If the company is not buying all the shares owned by the vendor or if although the vendor is selling all his shares he is retaining some other connection with the company – for example, a directorship or an appointment as consultant – it would seem unlikely that the transaction could benefit the company's trade, so the trade benefit test will probably not be satisfied.

However, there are exceptions; for example, where a company does not currently have the resources to buy out its retiring controlling shareholder completely but purchases as many of his shares as it can afford with the intention of buying the remainder where possible. In these circumstances, it may still be possible for the company to show that the main purpose is to benefit its trade. Also, the Board do not raise any objection if for sentimental reasons it is desired that a retiring director of a company should retain a small shareholding in it, not exceeding 5% of the issued share capital.

ANNEX

Applications for advance clearance under TA 1988 s 225

Procedure

If clearance under TA 1988 s 225 is desired the application should be sent to Inland Revenue, Central Registry, Room 28, New Wing, Somerset House, London WC2R 1LB. If clearance is also being sought under TA 1988 s 707 a single application may be made under both provisions and should be directed to the address given above with an extra copy of the application and enclosures. Such an application should open by stating clearly the provisions under which it is made and should be expanded to include any additional information needed for the application under the other provision.

Form of application – general

TA 1988 ss 219–229 contain conditions which must be satisfied before the tax treatment afforded by s 219 can apply. A comprehensive application which has regard to each of these conditions will remove the need for lengthy fact finding enquiries and enable the Board to come to a decision on the application with the minimum of delay.

To assist companies in preparing clearance applications under TA 1988 s 225 and to facilitate their consideration by the Board an outline of the basic information needed is given below. However, it is not an exhaustive list, and in giving the particulars of the relevant transactions required by s 225(2) the applicant must fully and accurately disclose all facts and circumstances material for the decision of the Board (s 225(5)).

In what follows, references to purchase of shares include references to repayment or redemption of shares.

It will be helpful if applications follow the order set out below, each item being expanded as necessary and any further information being added at the end.

Applications for clearance under TA 1988 s 225(1)(a)

It should be stated at the outset whether the purchase of shares is regarded as falling within TA 1988 s 219(1) by virtue of (a) or (b). If the purchasing company has previously made any application under s 225 it will be helpful if the Board's reference(s) can be quoted.

Purchase within TA 1988 s 219(1)(a)

1 *The company*

(a) the name of the company making the purchase;
(b) its Tax District and reference;
(c) confirmation that it is an unquoted company as defined in TA 1988 s 229(1);
(d) its status, that is, 'trading company' or 'holding company of a trading group' within the TA 1988 s 229(1) definitions or some other type of company not within the definitions.

2 *Groups*

Where the company is a member of a group (see below):

(a) the names of the group companies together with their tax references;
(b) a statement or diagram showing the shareholding interests of each group company in other group companies.

A group for the purpose of this paragraph is the largest 51% group to which the purchasing company belongs (TA 1988 s 222(9)), but the meaning of 'group' is extended, where appropriate, by TA 1988 s 222(1) and (12).

3 *The payment*

(a) details of the shares to be purchased, the name of their present owner, the purchase price and the method of payment;
(b) details of any other transactions between the company and the vendor at or about the same time;
(c) confirmation that the company's Articles of Association allow it to purchase its own shares.

4 *Shareholders*

(a) a list of the current shareholders in the purchasing company and where appropriate, in each company in a group as in 2 above, together with particulars (amount, class, dividend rights etc) of their current holdings;
(b) a statement of any relationships of the shareholders to each other;
(c) where the shareholder is the son or daughter of another shareholder, an indication that he or she is over 18 or else details of their age.

5 *Prior transactions*

Particulars of any prior transactions or rearrangements to be carried out in preparation for the purchase.

6 *Purpose and benefits*

A statement of the reasons for the purchase, the trading benefits expected and any other benefits expected to accrue, whether or not to the purchasing company.

7 *Conditions in TA 1988 s 219*

Confirmation together with all relevant information that the purchase etc does not form part of a scheme or arrangement the main purpose or one of the main purposes of which is to enable the owner of the shares to participate in the profits of the company without receiving a dividend, or the avoidance of tax. Confirmation that the vendor will receive no other payment from the company, or details of any such payment to be made.

8 *Conditions in TA 1988 ss 220–224*

- (a) the present residence status of the vendor and any intended change (TA 1988 s 220);
- (b) the Tax District, reference and National Insurance number of the vendor, or if not known his or her private address (TA 1988 s 220);
- (c) the period of beneficial ownership by the vendor of the shares to be purchased (TA 1988 s 220(5));
- (d) confirmation, if appropriate, that the vendor's interest will be 'substantially reduced' (TA 1988 s 221(1));
- (e) confirmation, if appropriate, that the combined interests as shareholders of the vendor and his 'associates' (see TA 1988 s 227) will be substantially reduced (TA 1988 s 221(2));
- (f) confirmation, if appropriate, that the vendor's interest as a shareholder in the group will be substantially reduced (TA 1988 s 222(1));
- (g) confirmation if appropriate, that the combined interests as shareholders in the group of the vendor and his associates will be substantially reduced (TA 1988 s 222(3));
- (h) confirmation that the vendor will not, immediately after the purchase, be 'connected with' (see TA 1988 s 228) the company making the purchase or with any company which is a member of the same group as that company (TA 1988 s 223(1));
- (j) confirmation that the purchase is not part of a scheme or arrangement within TA 1988 s 223(2).

9 *Accounts and other financial information*

The application should be accompanied by:

- (a) copies of the latest available financial statements for the purchasing company and for any group companies (see paragraph 2 above), and in the case of a group the financial statements for the group;
- (b) a note of any material relevant changes since the balance sheet date or confirmation that there are none; and
- (c) details of any loan or current account which the vendor maintains with the company or with any group company.

18 STATEMENT OF PRACTICE SP2/82 (ORIGINAL VERSION)

Section [219(1)(a)][1]

1 Section [219(1)(a)] provides that references in the Corporation Tax Acts to distributions of a company shall not include references to a payment made by a company on the redemption, repayment or purchase of its own shares if, among other conditions, the redemption, repayment or purchase is made wholly or mainly for the purpose of benefiting a trade carried on by the company or by any of its 75% subsidiaries.

2 This test indicates that the sole or main purpose of the transaction is to be to benefit a trade of a relevant company and not, for example, to benefit the vending shareholder (although he usually will also benefit) nor some wider commercial purpose to which he may put the payment he receives nor any business purpose of a relevant company itself if it is not a trade, such as an investment activity which it may also carry on.

3 If the problem being resolved by the transaction is a disagreement over the management of the company, the main purpose may nonetheless be to benefit a trade if, as will usually be the case with a trading company, the disagreement has or can reasonably be expected to have an adverse effect on the running of the trade. It would not be so, however if, exceptionally, the disagreement were, for example, over the question whether the company should discontinue trading and become an investment company and the shareholder being bought out advocated the continuance of trading.

4 More generally, with rare exceptions of the kind just mentioned, since it will normally be unsatisfactory to retain an unwilling shareholder it is expected that the condition will be shown to be satisfied where, after taking into account the interests of any associates, the vending shareholder is genuinely giving up his entire interest of all kinds in the company. The case of a boardroom disagreement has already been mentioned; other examples where this might happen are:

(a) an outside shareholder has provided equity finance (whether or not with the expectation of redemption or sale to the company); he is now withdrawing his investment;
(b) the proprietor of a company is retiring to make way for new management;
(c) a shareholder has died leaving shares in his estate and his personal representatives or the beneficiaries do not wish to keep them.

5 Where a shareholder is only reducing (by 25% or more) his proportionate interest in shares and profits, or retaining some other interest, it is less likely that the condition will be satisfied. It cannot, for example, then usually be argued that the purpose is to remove his continued unwilling presence which could otherwise damage the trade. But the condition might still be satisfied

1 As originally issued this statement contained references to FA 1982 s 53 and Sch 9. These references have been updated to TA 1988.

where the intention was that his entire interest should cease but this was to be achieved by more than one transaction (for example, because the company could not afford to buy all his shares at one time): or where the interest he retained was minimal and kept only for sentimental reasons.

Section [219(1)(b)]

6 'substantially the whole' means almost all.

[Section 222(12)]

7 In the context of Section [410 ICTA 1988], the Board expressed their views on the meaning of the word 'arrangements' in SP5/80 (dated 26 March 1980). Insofar as relevant, what is said there applies also to the meaning of the word 'arrangements' in [section 222(12)].

[Section 223(3)]

8 The coming into ownership of shares, whether by personal representatives or by beneficiaries under a will or an intestacy is not a transaction within the meaning of this sub-paragraph. Where the relevant death occurred after the purchase referred to in [section 223(3)], a subsequent sale of those shares by the personal representatives or beneficiary could not of itself cause [section 223(3)] to apply.

[Section 225]

9 This [section] provides a clearance procedure. Guidance is attached on where applications should be sent and the form they should take.

[Section 226(5)]

10 Where trustees are made associates of a person by [section 226(5)] it is only their interest in their capacity as trustees of the trust there mentioned which are taken into account as a result of that sub-[section] for the purposes of the [Act] (for example, in [section 221(2, 3)] and [section 228(7)]), not any personal interests they may have or any interests they may have as trustees of other trusts.

[Section 227(7)]

11 Unless there is other reason to regard this as applicable, this provision will not be regarded as applying to the normal relationship between an employee and someone set over him in a company.

Appendix Two

SELECTED LEGISLATION

COMPANY LAW

Purchase and redemption of shares

COMPANIES ACT 1985

Section 143 – general rule against company acquiring own shares

1 Subject to the following provisions, a company limited by shares or limited by guarantee and having a share capital shall not acquire its own shares, whether by purchase, subscription or otherwise.

2 If a company purports to act in contravention of this section, the company is liable to a fine, and every officer of the company who is in default is liable to imprisonment or a fine, or both; and the purported acquisition is void.

3 A company limited by shares may acquire any of its own fully paid shares otherwise than for valuable consideration; and subsection (1) does not apply in relation to:

(a) the redemption or purchase of shares in accordance with Chapter VII of this Part,

. . .

Section 159 – power to issue redeemable shares

1 Subject to the provisions of this Chapter, a company limited by shares or limited by guarantee and having a share capital may, if authorised to do so by its articles, issue shares which are to be redeemed or are liable to be redeemed at the option of the company or the shareholder.

2 No redeemable shares may be issued at a time when there are no issued shares of the company which are not redeemable.

3 Redeemable shares may not be redeemed unless they are fully paid; and the terms of redemption must provide for payment on redemption.

Section 160 – financing etc of redemption

1 Subject to the next subsection and to sections 171 (private companies redeeming or purchasing own shares out of capital) and 178(4) (terms of redemption or purchase enforceable in a winding up):

(a) redeemable shares may only be redeemed out of distributable profits of the company or out of the proceeds of a fresh issue of shares made for the purposes of the redemption; and
(b) any premium payable on redemption must be paid out of distributable profits of the company.

2 If the redeemable shares were issued at a premium, any premium payable on their redemption may be paid out of the proceeds of a fresh issue of shares made for the purposes of the redemption, up to an amount equal to:

(a) the aggregate of the premiums received by the company on the issue of the shares redeemed, or
(b) the current amount of the company's share premium account (including any sum transferred to that account in respect of premiums on the new shares),

whichever is the less; and in that case the amount of the company's share premium account shall be reduced by a sum corresponding (or by sums in the aggregate corresponding) to the amount of any payment made by virtue of this subsection out of the proceeds of the issue of the new shares.

3 Subject to the following provisions of this Chapter, redemption of shares may be effected on such terms and in such manner as may be provided by the company's articles.

4) Shares redeemed under this section shall be treated as cancelled on redemption, and the amount of the company's issued share capital shall be diminished by the nominal value of those shares accordingly; but the redemption of shares by a company is not to be taken as reducing the amount of the company's authorised share capital.

5 Without prejudice to subsection (4), where a company is about to redeem shares, it has power to issue shares up to the nominal value of the shares to be redeemed as if those shares had never been issued.

Section 162 – power of company to purchase own shares

1 Subject to the following provisions of this Chapter, a company limited by shares or limited by guarantee and having a share capital may, if authorised to do so by its articles, purchase its own shares (including any redeemable shares).

2 Sections 159 to 161 apply to the purchase by a company under this section of its own shares as they apply to the redemption of redeemable shares, save that the terms and manner of purchase need not be determined by the articles as required by section 160(3).

3 A company may not under this section purchase its shares if as a result of the purchase there would no longer be any member of the company holding shares other than redeemable shares.

Section 163 – definitions of 'off-market' and 'market' purchase

1 A purchase by a company of its own shares is 'off-market' if the shares either:

(a) are purchased otherwise than on a recognised investment exchange, or

. . .

Section 164 – authority for off-market purchase

1 A company may only make an off-market purchase of its own shares in pursuance of a contract approved in advance in accordance with this section or under section 165 below.

2 The terms of the proposed contract must be authorised by a special resolution of the company before the contract is entered into; and the following subsections apply with respect to that authority and to resolutions conferring it.

3 Subject to the next subsection, the authority may be varied, revoked or from time to time renewed by special resolution of the company.

. . .

5 A special resolution to confer, vary, revoke or renew authority is not effective if any member of the company holding shares to which the resolution relates exercises the voting rights carried by any of those shares in voting on the resolution and the resolution would not have been passed if he had not done so.

For this purpose:

(a) a member who holds shares to which the resolution relates is regarded as exercising the voting rights carried by those shares not only if he votes in respect of them on a poll on the question whether the resolution shall be passed, but also if he votes on the resolution otherwise than on a poll;
(b) notwithstanding anything in the company's articles, any member of the company may demand a poll on that question; and
(c) a vote and a demand for a poll by a person as proxy for a member are the same respectively as a vote and a demand by the member.

6 Such a resolution is not effective for the purposes of this section unless (if the proposed contract is in writing) a copy of the contract or (if not) a written memorandum of its terms is available for inspection by members of the company both:

(a) at the company's registered office for not less than 15 days ending with the date of the meeting at which the resolution is passed, and
(b) at the meeting itself.

A memorandum of contract terms so made available must include the names of any members holding shares to which the contract relates; and a copy of the contract so made available must have annexed to it a written memorandum specifying any such names which do not appear in the contract itself.

7 A company may agree to a variation of an existing contract so approved, but only if the variation is authorised by a special resolution of the company before it is agreed to; and subsections (3) to (6) above apply to the authority for a proposed variation as they apply to the authority for a proposed contract, save that a copy of the original contract or (as the case may require) a memorandum of its terms, together with any variations previously made, must also be available for inspection in accordance with subsection (6).

Section 165 – authority for contingent purchase contract

1 A contingent purchase contract is a contract entered into by a company and relating to any of its shares:

(a) which does not amount to a contract to purchase those shares, but
(b) under which the company may (subject to any conditions) become entitled or obliged to purchase those shares.

2 A company may only make a purchase of its own shares in pursuance of a contingent purchase contract if the contract is approved in advance by a special resolution of the company before the contract is entered into; and subsections (3) to (7) of section 164 apply to the contract and its terms.

Section 167 – assignment or release of company's right to purchase own shares

1 The rights of a company under a contract approved under section 164 or 165 . . . are not capable of being assigned.

2 An agreement by a company to release its rights under a contract approved under section 164 or 165 is void unless the terms of the release agreement are approved in advance by a special resolution of the company before the agreement is entered into; and subsections (3) to (7) of section 164 apply to approval for a proposed release agreement as to authority for a proposed variation of an existing contract.

Section 168 – payments apart from purchase price to be made out of distributable profits

1 A payment made by a company in consideration of:

(a) acquiring any right with respect to the purchase of its own shares in pursuance of a contract approved under section 165,
(b) the variation of a contract approved under section 164 or 165, or

(c) the release of any of the company's obligations with respect to the purchase of any of its own shares under a contract approved under section 164 or 165 . . .

must be made out of the company's distributable profits.

2 If the requirements of subsection (1) are not satisfied in relation to a contract:

(a) in a case within paragraph (a) of the subsection, no purchase by the company of its own shares in pursuance of that contract is lawful under this Chapter,
(b) in a case within paragraph (b), no such purchase following the variation is lawful under this Chapter, and
(c) in a case within paragraph (c), the purported release is void.

Section 169 – disclosure by company of purchase of own shares

1 Within the period of 28 days beginning with the date on which any shares purchased by a company under this Chapter are delivered to it, the company shall deliver to the registrar of companies for registration a return in the prescribed form stating with respect to shares of each class purchased the number and nominal value of those shares and the date on which they were delivered to the company.

. . .

3 Particulars of shares delivered to the company on different dates and under different contracts may be included in a single return to the registrar; and in such a case the amount required to be stated under subsection (2)(a) is the aggregate amount paid by the company for all the shares to which the return relates.

4 Where a company enters into a contract approved under section 164 or 165, . . . the company shall keep at its registered office:

(a) if the contract is in writing, a copy of it; and
(b) if not, a memorandum of its terms,

from the conclusion of the contract until the end of the period of ten years beginning with the date on which the purchase of all the shares in pursuance of the contract is completed or (as the case may be) the date on which the contract otherwise determines.

5 Every copy and memorandum so required to be kept shall be open to inspection without charge:

(a) by any member of the company, . . .

. . .

6 If default is made in delivering to the registrar any return required by this section, every officer of the company who is in default is liable to a fine and, for continued contravention, to a daily default fine.

7 If default is made in complying with subsection (4), or if an inspection required under subsection (5) is refused, the company and every officer of it who is in default is liable to a fine and, for continued contravention, to a daily default fine.

8 In the case of a refusal of an inspection required under subsection (5) of a copy or memorandum, the court may by order compel an immediate inspection of it.

9 The obligation of a company under subsection (4) to keep a copy of any contract or (as the case may be) a memorandum of its terms applies to any variation of the contract so long as it applies to the contract.

Section 170 – the capital redemption reserve

1 Where under this Chapter shares of a company are redeemed or purchased wholly out of the company's profits, the amount by which the company's issued share capital is diminished in accordance with section 160(4) on cancellation of the shares redeemed or purchased shall be transferred to a reserve, called 'the capital redemption reserve'.

2 If the shares are redeemed or purchased wholly or partly out of the proceeds of a fresh issue and the aggregate amount of those proceeds is less than the aggregate nominal value of the shares redeemed or purchased, the amount of the difference shall be transferred to the capital redemption reserve.

3 But subsection (2) does not apply if the proceeds of the fresh issue are applied by the company in making a redemption or purchase of its own shares in addition to a payment out of capital under section 171.

4 The provisions of this Act relating to the reduction of a company's share capital apply as if the capital redemption reserve were paid up share capital of the company, except that the reserve may be applied by the company in paying up its unissued shares to be allotted to members of the company as fully paid bonus shares.

Section 171 – power of private companies to redeem or purchase own shares out of capital

1 Subject to the following provisions of this Chapter, a private company limited by shares or limited by guarantee and having a share capital may, if so authorised by its articles, make a payment in respect of the redemption or purchase under section 160 or (as the case may be) section 162, of its own shares otherwise than out of its distributable profits or the proceeds of a fresh issue of shares.

2 References below in this Chapter to payment out of capital are (subject to subsection (6)) to any payment so made, whether or not it would be regarded apart from this section as a payment out of capital.

3 The payment which may (if authorised in accordance with the following provisions of this Chapter) be made by a company out of capital in

respect of the redemption or purchase of its own shares is such an amount as, taken together with:

(a) any available profits of the company, and
(b) the proceeds of any fresh issue of shares made for the purposes of the redemption or purchase,

is equal to the price of redemption or purchase; and the payment permissible under this subsection is referred to below in this Chapter as the permissible capital payment for the shares.

4 Subject to subsection (6), if the permissible capital payment for shares redeemed or purchased is less than their nominal amount, the amount of the difference shall be transferred to the company's capital redemption reserve.

5 Subject to subsection (6), if the permissible capital payment is greater than the nominal amount of the shares redeemed or purchased:

(a) the amount of any capital redemption reserve, share premium account or fully paid share capital of the company, and
(b) any amount representing unrealised profits of the company for the time being standing to the credit of any reserve maintained by the company in accordance with paragraph 34 of Schedule 4 (revaluation reserve),

may be reduced by a sum not exceeding (or by sums not in the aggregate exceeding) the amount by which the permissible capital payment exceeds the nominal amount of the shares.

6 Where the proceeds of a fresh issue are applied by a company in making any redemption or purchase of its own shares in addition to a payment out of capital under this section, the references in subsections (4) and (5) to the permissible capital payment are to be read as referring to the aggregate of that payment and those proceeds.

Section 172 – availability of profits for purposes of s 171

1 The reference in section 171(3)(a) to available profits of the company is to the company's profits which are available for distribution (within the meaning of Part VIII); but the question whether a company has any profits so available and the amount of any such profits are to be determined for purposes of that section in accordance with the following subsections, instead of sections 270 to 275 in that Part.

2 Subject to the next subsection, that question is to be determined by reference to:

(a) profits, losses, assets and liabilities,
(b) provisions of any of the kinds mentioned in paragraphs 88 and 89 of Schedule 4 (depreciation, diminution in value of assets, retentions to meet liabilities, etc), and
(c) share capital and reserves (including undistributable reserves),

as stated in the relevant accounts for determining the permissible capital payment for shares.

3 The relevant accounts for this purpose are such accounts, prepared as at any date within the period for determining the amount of the permissible capital payment, as are necessary to enable a reasonable judgment to be made as to the amounts of any of the items mentioned in subsection (2)(a) to (c) above.

4 For purposes of determining the amount of the permissible capital payment for shares, the amount of the company's available profits (if any) determined in accordance with subsections (2) and (3) is treated as reduced by the amount of any distributions lawfully made by the company after the date of the relevant accounts and before the end of the period for determining the amount of that payment.

5 The reference in subsection (4) to distributions lawfully made by the company includes:

(a) financial assistance lawfully given out of distributable profits in a case falling within section 154 or 155,
(b) any payment lawfully made by the company in respect of the purchase by it of any shares in the company (except a payment lawfully made otherwise than out of distributable profits), and
(c) a payment of any description specified in section 168(1) lawfully made by the company.

6 References in this section to the period for determining the amount of the permissible capital payment for shares are to the period of three months ending with the date on which the statutory declaration of the directors purporting to specify the amount of that payment is made in accordance with subsection (3) of the section next following.

Section 173 – conditions for payment out of capital

1 Subject to any order of the court under section 177, a payment out of capital by a private company for the redemption or purchase of its own shares is not lawful unless the requirements of this and the next two sections are satisfied.

2 The payment out of capital must be approved by a special resolution of the company.

3 The company's directors must make a statutory declaration specifying the amount of the permissible capital payment for the shares in question and stating that, having made full inquiry into the affairs and prospects of the company, they have formed the opinion:

(a) as regards its initial situation immediately following the date on which the payment out of capital is proposed to be made, that there will be no grounds on which the company could then be found unable to pay its debts, and
(b) as regards its prospects for the year immediately following that date,

that, having regard to their intentions with respect to the management of the company's business during that year and to the amount and character of the financial resources which will in their view be available to the company during that year, the company will be able to continue to carry on business as a going concern (and will accordingly be able to pay its debts as they fall due) throughout that year.

4 In forming their opinion for purposes of subsection (3)(a), the directors shall take into account the same liabilities (including prospective and contingent liabilities) as would be relevant under section 122 of the Insolvency Act (winding up by the court) to the question whether a company is unable to pay its debts.

5 The directors' statutory declaration must be in the prescribed form and contain such information with respect to the nature of the company's business as may be prescribed, and must in addition have annexed to it a report addressed to the directors by the company's auditors stating that:

(a) they have inquired into the company's state of affairs; and
(b) the amount specified in the declaration as the permissible capital payment for the shares in question is in their view properly determined in accordance with sections 171 and 172; and
(c) they are not aware of anything to indicate that the opinion expressed by the directors in the declaration as to any of the matters mentioned in subsection (3) is unreasonable in all the circumstances.

6 A director who makes a declaration under this section without having reasonable grounds for the opinion expressed in the declaration is liable to imprisonment or a fine, or both.

Section 174 – procedure for special resolution under s 173

1 The resolution required by section 173 must be passed on, or within the week immediately following, the date on which the directors make the statutory declaration required by that section; and the payment out of capital must be made no earlier than five nor more than seven weeks after the date of the resolution.

2 The resolution is ineffective if any member of the company holding shares to which the resolution relates exercises the voting rights carried by any of those shares in voting on the resolution and the resolution would not have been passed if he had not done so.

3 For purposes of subsection (2), a member who holds such shares is to be regarded as exercising the voting rights carried by them in voting on the resolution not only if he votes in respect of them on a poll on the question whether the resolution shall be passed, but also if he votes on the resolution otherwise than on a poll; and, notwithstanding anything in a company's articles, any member of the company may demand a poll on that question.

4 The resolution is ineffective unless the statutory declaration and auditors' report required by the section are available for inspection by

members of the company at the meeting at which the resolution is passed.

5 For purposes of this section a vote and a demand for a poll by a person as proxy for a member are the same (respectively) as a vote and demand by the member.

Section 175 – publicity for proposed payment out of capital

1 Within the week immediately following the date of the resolution for payment out of capital the company must cause to be published in the Gazette a notice:

(a) stating that the company has approved a payment out of capital for the purpose of acquiring its own shares by redemption or purchase or both (as the case may be);
(b) specifying the amount of the permissible capital payment for the shares in question and the date of the resolution under section 173;
(c) stating that the statutory declaration of the directors and the auditors' report required by that section are available for inspection at the company's registered office; and
(d) stating that any creditor of the company may at any time within the five weeks immediately following the date of the resolution for payment out of capital apply to the court under section 176 for an order prohibiting the payment.

2 Within the week immediately following the date of the resolution the company must also either cause a notice to the same effect as that required by subsection (1) to be published in an appropriate national newspaper or give notice in writing to that effect to each of its creditors.

3 'An appropriate national newspaper' means a newspaper circulating throughout England and Wales (in the case of a company registered in England and Wales), and a newspaper circulating throughout Scotland (in the case of a company registered in Scotland).

4 References below in this section to the first notice date are to the day on which the company first publishes the notice required by subsection (1) or first publishes or gives the notice required by subsection (2) (whichever is the earlier).

5 Not later than the first notice date the company must deliver to the registrar of companies a copy of the statutory declaration of the directors and of the auditors' report required by section 173.

6 The statutory declaration and auditors' report:

(a) shall be kept at the company's registered office throughout the period beginning with the first notice date and ending five weeks after the date of the resolution for payment out of capital, and
(b) shall be open to the inspection of any member or creditor of the company without charge.

7 If an inspection required under subsection (6) is refused, the company and every officer of it who is in default is liable to a fine and, for continued contravention, to a daily default fine.

8 In the case of refusal of an inspection required under subsection (6) of a declaration or report, the court may by order compel an immediate inspection of that declaration or report.

Section 176 – objections by company's members or creditors

1 Where a private company passes a special resolution approving for purposes of this Chapter any payment out of capital for the redemption or purchase of any of its shares:

(a) any member of the company other than one who consented to or voted in favour of the resolution; and
(b) any creditor of the company,

may within five weeks of the date on which the resolution was passed apply to the court for cancellation of the resolution.

2 The application may be made on behalf of the persons entitled to make it by such one or more of their number as they may appoint in writing for the purpose.

3 If an application is made, the company shall:

(a) forthwith give notice in the prescribed form of that fact to the registrar of companies; and
(b) within 15 days from the making of any order of the court on the hearing of the application, or such longer period as the court may by order direct, deliver an office copy of the order to the registrar.

4 A company which fails to comply with subsection (3), and any officer of it who is in default, is liable to a fine and for continued contravention, to a daily default fine.

Section 177 – powers of court on application under section 176

1 On the hearing of an application under section 176 the court may, if it thinks fit, adjourn the proceedings in order that an arrangement may be made to the court's satisfaction for the purchase of the interests of dissentient members or for the protection of dissentient creditors (as the case may be); and the court may give such directions and make such orders as it thinks expedient for facilitating or carrying into effect any such arrangement.

2 Without prejudice to its powers under subsection (1), the court shall make an order on such terms and conditions as it thinks fit either confirming or cancelling the resolution; and, if the court confirms the resolution, it may in particular by order alter or extend any date or period of time specified in the resolution or in any provision in this Chapter which applies to the redemption or purchase of shares to which the resolution refers.

3 The court's order may, if the court thinks fit, provide for the purchase by the company of the shares of any of its members and for the reduction accordingly of the company's capital, and may make such alterations in the company's memorandum and articles as may be required in consequence of that provision.

4 If the court's order requires the company not to make any, or any specified, alteration in its memorandum or articles, the company has not then power without leave of the court to make any such alteration in breach of the requirement.

5 An alteration in the memorandum or articles made by virtue of an order under this section, if not made by resolution of the company, is of the same effect as if duly made by resolution; and this Act applies accordingly to the memorandum or articles as so altered.

Section 178 – effect of company's failure to redeem or purchase

1 This section has effect where a company has, on or after 15 June 1982:

(a) issued shares on terms that they are or are liable to be redeemed, or
(b) agreed to purchase any of its own shares.

2 The company is not liable in damages in respect of any failure on its part to redeem or purchase any of the shares.

3 Subsection (2) is without prejudice to any right of the holder of the shares other than his right to sue the company for damages in respect of its failure; but the court shall not grant an order for specific performance of the terms of redemption or purchase if the company shows that it is unable to meet the costs of redeeming or purchasing the shares in question out of distributable profits.

4 If the company is wound up and at the commencement of the winding up any of the shares have not been redeemed or purchased, the terms of redemption or purchase may be enforced against the company; and when shares are redeemed or purchased under this subsection, they are treated as cancelled.

5 However, subsection (4) does not apply if:

(a) the terms provided for the redemption or purchase to take place at a date later than that of the commencement of the winding up, or
(b) during the period beginning with the date on which the redemption or purchase was to have taken place and ending with the commencement of the winding up the company could not at any time have lawfully made a distribution equal in value to the price at which the shares were to have been redeemed or purchased.

6 There shall be paid in priority to any amount which the company is liable under subsection (4) to pay in respect of any shares:

(a) all other debts and liabilities of the company (other than any due to members in their character as such),
(b) if other shares carry rights (whether as to capital or as to income) which are preferred to the rights as to capital attaching to the first-mentioned shares, any amount due in satisfaction of those preferred rights;

but, subject to that, any such amount shall be paid in priority to any amounts due to members in satisfaction of their rights (whether as to capital or income) as members.

Section 181 – definitions for Chapter VII

In this Chapter:

(a) 'distributable profits', in relation to the making of any payment by a company, means those profits out of which it could lawfully make a distribution (within the meaning given by section 263(2)) equal in value to the payment, and
(b) 'permissible capital payment' means the payment permitted by section 171;

and references to payment out of capital are to be construed in accordance with section 171.

Disclosure Requirements

COMPANIES ACT 1985, SCHEDULE 7

Paragraph 7

This Part of this Schedule applies where shares in a company:

(a) are purchased by the company or are acquired by it . . . in pursuance of section 143(3) of this Act (acquisition of own shares by company limited by shares),

. . .

Paragraph 8

The directors' report with respect to a financial year shall state:

(a) the number and nominal value of the shares so purchased, the aggregate amount of the consideration paid by the company for such shares and the reasons for their purchase;

(b) the number and nominal value of the shares so acquired by the company, . . . during the financial year;

(c) the maximum number and nominal value of shares which, having been so acquired by the company, . . . are held at any time by the company . . . during that year;

(d) the number and nominal value of the shares so acquired by the company, which are disposed of by the company . . . during that year;

(e) where the number and nominal value of the shares of any particular description are stated in pursuance of any of the preceding sub-paragraphs, the percentage of the called-up share capital which shares of that description represent;

. . .

(g) where any of the shares have been disposed of by the company . . . for money or money's worth the amount or value of the consideration in each case.

Issue of New Shares

Companies Act 1985

Section 80 – authority of company required for certain allotments

1 The directors of a company shall not exercise any power of the company to allot relevant securities, unless they are, in accordance with this section or section 80A, authorised to do so by:

(a) the company in general meeting; or
(b) the company's articles.

2 In this section 'relevant securities' means:

(a) shares in the company other than shares shown in the memorandum to have been taken by the subscribers to it or shares allotted in pursuance of an employees' share scheme, and
(b) any right to subscribe for, or to convert any security into, shares in the company (other than shares so allotted);

and a reference to the allotment of relevant securities includes the grant of such a right but (subject to subsection (6) below), not the allotment of shares pursuant to such a right.

3 Authority under this section may be given for a particular exercise of the power or for its exercise generally, and may be unconditional or subject to conditions.

4 The authority must state the maximum amount of relevant securities that may be allotted under it and the date on which it will expire, which must be not more than five years from whichever is relevant of the following dates:

(a) in the case of an authority contained in the company's articles at the time of its original incorporation, the date of that incorporation; and
(b) in any other case, the date on which the resolution is passed by virtue of which the authority is given;

but such an authority (including an authority contained in the articles) may be previously revoked or varied by the company in general meeting.

5 The authority may be renewed or further renewed by the company in general meeting for a further period not exceeding five years; but the resolution must state (or restate) the amount of relevant securities which may be allotted under the authority or, as the case may be, the amount remaining to be allotted under it, and must specify the date on which the renewed authority will expire.

6 In relation to authority under this section for the grant of such rights as are mentioned in subsection (2)(b), the reference in subsection (4) (as also the corresponding reference in subsection (5)) to the maximum amount of relevant securities that may be allotted under the authority is to the maximum amount of shares which may be allotted pursuant to the rights.

7 The directors may allot relevant securities, notwithstanding that authority under this section has expired, if they are allotted in pursuance of an offer or agreement made by the company before the authority expired and the authority allowed it to make an offer or agreement which would or might require relevant securities to be allotted after the authority expired.

8 A resolution of a company to give, vary, revoke or renew such an authority may, notwithstanding that it alters the company's articles, be an ordinary resolution; but it is in any case subject to section 380 of this Act (copy to be forwarded to registrar within 15 days).

9 A director who knowingly and wilfully contravenes, or permits or authorises a contravention of, this section is liable to a fine.

10 Nothing in this section affects the validity of any allotment.

11 This section does not apply to any allotment of relevant securities by a company, other than a public company registered as such on its original incorporation, if it is made in pursuance of an offer or agreement made before the earlier of the following two dates:

(a) the date of the holding of the first general meeting of the company after its registration or re-registration as a public company, and
(b) 22 June 1982;

but any resolution to give, vary or revoke an authority for the purposes of section 14 of the Companies Act 1980 or this section has effect for those purposes if passed at any time after the end of April 1980.

Secion 80A – election by private company as to duration of authority

1 A private company may elect (by elective resolution in accordance with section 379A) that the provisions of this section shall apply, instead of the provisions of section 80(4) and (5), in relation to the giving or renewal, after the election, of an authority under that section.

2 The authority must state the maximum amount of relevant securities that may be allotted under it and may be given:

(a) for an indefinite period, or
(b) for a fixed period, in which case it must state the date on which it will expire.

3 In either case an authority (including an authority contained in the articles) may be revoked or varied by the company in general meeting.

4 An authority given for a fixed period may be renewed or further renewed by the company in general meeting.

5 A resolution renewing an authority:

(a) must state, or re-state, the amount of relevant securities which may be allotted under the authority or, as the case may be, the amount remaining to be allotted under it, and
(b) must state whether the authority is renewed for an indefinite period or for a fixed period, in which case it must state the date on which the renewed authority will expire.

6 The references in this section to the maximum amount of relevant securities that may be allotted shall be construed in accordance with section 80(6).

7 If an election under this section ceases to have effect, an authority then in force which was given for an indefinite period or for a fixed period of more than five years:

(a) if given five years or more before the election ceases to have effect, shall expire forthwith, and
(b) otherwise, shall have effect as if it had been given for a fixed period of five years.

Section 81 – restriction on public offers by private company

1 A private limited company (other than a company limited by guarantee and not having a share capital) commits an offence if it:

(a) offers to the public (whether for cash or otherwise) any shares in or debentures of the company; or
(b) allots or agrees to allot (whether for cash or otherwise) any shares in or debentures of the company with a view to all or any of those shares or debentures being offered for sale to the public (within the meaning given to that expression by sections 58 to 60).

2 A company guilty of an offence under this section, and any officer of it who is in default, is liable to a fine.

3 Nothing in this section affects the validity of any allotment or sale of shares or debentures, or of any agreement to allot or sell shares or debentures.

Section 88 – return as to allotments, etc

1 This section applies to a company limited by shares and to a company limited by guarantee and having a share capital.

2 When such a company makes an allotment of its shares, the company shall within one month thereafter deliver to the registrar of companies for registration:

(a) a return of the allotments (in the prescribed form) stating the number and nominal amount of the shares comprised in the allotment, the names and addresses of the allottees, and the amount (if any) paid or due and payable on each share, whether on account of the nominal value of the share or by way of premium; and
(b) in the case of shares allotted as fully or partly paid up otherwise than in cash:
(i) a contract in writing constituting the title of the allottee to the allotment together with any contract of sale, or for services or other consideration in respect of which that allotment was made (such contracts being duly stamped), and
(ii) a return stating the number and nominal amount of shares so allotted, the extent to which they are to be treated as paid up, and the consideration for which they have been allotted.

3 Where such a contract as above mentioned is not reduced to writing, the company shall within one month after the allotment deliver to the registrar of companies for registration the prescribed particulars of the contract stamped with the same stamp duty as would have been payable if the contract had been reduced to writing.

4 Those particulars are deemed an instrument within the meaning of the Stamp Act 1891; and the registrar may, as a condition of filing the particulars, require that the duty payable on them be adjudicated under section 12 of that Act.

5 If default is made in complying with this section, every officer of the company who is in default is liable to a fine and, for continued contravention, to a daily default fine, but subject as follows.

6 In the case of default in delivering to the registrar within one month after the allotment any document required by this section to be delivered, the company, or any officer liable for the default, may apply to the court for relief; and the court, if satisfied that the omission to deliver the document was accidental or due to inadvertence, or that it is just and equitable to grant relief, may make an order extending the time for the delivery of the document for such period as the court thinks proper.

Section 89 – offers to shareholders to be on pre-emptive basis

1 Subject to the provisions of this section and the seven sections next following, a company proposing to allot equity securities (defined in section 94):

(a) shall not allot any of them on any terms to a person unless it has made an offer to each person who holds relevant shares or relevant employee shares to allot to him on the same or more favourable terms a proportion of those securities which is as nearly as practicable equal to the proportion in nominal value held by him of the aggregate of relevant shares and relevant employee shares, and
(b) shall not allot any of those securities to a person unless the period during which any such offer may be accepted has expired or the company has received notice of the acceptance or refusal of every offer so made.

2 Subsection (3) below applies to any provision of a company's memorandum or articles which requires the company, when proposing to allot equity securities consisting of relevant shares of any particular class, not to allot those securities on any terms unless it has complied with the condition that it makes such an offer as is described in subsection (1) to each person who holds relevant shares or relevant employee shares of that class.

3 If in accordance with a provision to which this subsection applies:

(a) a company makes an offer to allot securities to such a holder, and
(b) he or anyone in whose favour he has renounced his right to their allotment accepts the offer,

subsection (1) does not apply to the allotment of those securities, and the company may allot them accordingly; but this is without prejudice to the application of subsection (1) in any other case.

4 Subsection (1) does not apply to a particular allotment of equity securities if these are, or are to be, wholly or partly paid up otherwise than in cash; and securities which a company has offered to allot to a holder of relevant shares or relevant employee shares may be allotted to him, or anyone in whose favour he has renounced his right to their allotment, without contravening subsection (1)(b).

5 Subsection (1) does not apply to the allotment of securities which would, apart from a renunciation or assignment of the right to their allotment, be held under an employees' share scheme.

Section 90 – communication of pre-emption offers to shareholders

1 This section has effect as to the manner in which offers required by section 89(1), or by a provision to which section 89(3) applies, are to be made to holders of a company's shares.

2 Subject to the following subsections, an offer shall be in writing and shall be made to a holder of shares either personally or by sending it by post (that is to say, prepaying and posting a letter containing the offer) to him or to his registered address or, if he has no registered address in the United Kingdom, to the address in the United Kingdom supplied by him to the company for the giving of notice to him.

If sent by post, the offer is deemed to be made at the time at which the letter would be delivered in the ordinary course of post.

3 Where shares are held by two or more persons jointly, the offer may be made to the joint holder first named in the register of members in respect of the shares.

4 In the case of a holder's death or bankruptcy, the offer may be made:

(a) by sending it by post in a prepaid letter addressed to the persons claiming to be entitled to the shares in consequence of the death or bankruptcy by name, or by the title of representatives of the deceased, or trustee of the bankrupt, or by any like description, at the address in the United Kingdom supplied for the purpose by those so claiming, or
(b) (until such an address has been so supplied) by giving the notice in any manner in which it might have been given if the death or bankruptcy had not occurred.

5 If the holder:

(a) has no registered address in the United Kingdom and has not given to the company an address in the United Kingdom for the service of notices on him, or
(b) is the holder of a share warrant,

the offer may be made by causing it, or a notice specifying where a copy of it can be obtained or inspected, to be published in the *Gazette*.

6 The offer must state a period of not less than 21 days during which it may be accepted; and the offer shall not be withdrawn before the end of that period.

7 This section does not invalidate a provision to which section 89(3) applies by reason that that provision requires or authorises an offer under it to be made in contravention of any of subsections (1) to (6) above; but, to the extent that the provision requires or authorises such an offer to be so made, it is of no effect.

Section 91 – exclusion of ss 89, 90 by private company

1 Section 89(1), section 90(1) to (5) or section 90(6) may, as applying to allotments by a private company of equity securities or to such allotments of a particular description, be excluded by a provision contained in the memorandum or articles of that company.

2 A requirement or authority contained in the memorandum or articles of a private company, if it is inconsistent with any of those subsections, has effect as a provision excluding that subsection; but a provision to which section 89(3) applies is not to be treated as inconsistent with section 89(1).

Section 92 – consequences of contravening sections 89, 90

1 If there is a contravention of section 89(1), or of section 90(1) to (5) or section 90(6), or of a provision to which section 89(3) applies, the company, and every officer of it who knowingly authorised or permitted the contravention, are jointly and severally liable to compensate any person to whom an offer should have been made under the subsection or provision contravened for any loss, damage, costs or expenses which the person has sustained or incurred by reason of the contravention.

2 However, no proceedings to recover any such loss, damage, costs or expenses shall be commenced after the expiration of 2 years from the delivery to the registrar of companies of the return of allotments in question or, where equity securities other than shares are granted, from the date of the grant.

Section 93 – saving for other restrictions as to offers

1 Sections 89 to 92 are without prejudice to any enactment by virtue of which a company is prohibited (whether generally or in specified circumstances) from offering or allotting equity securities to any person.

2 Where a company cannot by virtue of such an enactment offer or allot equity securities to a holder of relevant shares or relevant employee shares, those sections have effect as if the shares held by that holder were not relevant shares or relevant employee shares.

Section 94 – definitions for sections 89–96

1 The following subsections apply for the interpretation of sections 89 to 96.

2 'Equity security', in relation to a company, means a relevant share in the company (other than a share shown in the memorandum to have been taken by a subscriber to the memorandum or a bonus share), or a right to subscribe for, or to convert securities into, relevant shares in the company.

3 A reference to the allotment of equity securities or of equity securities consisting of relevant shares of a particular class includes the grant of a right to subscribe for, or to convert any securities into, relevant shares in the company or (as the case may be) relevant shares of a particular class; but such a reference does not include the allotment of any relevant shares pursuant to such a right.

4 'Relevant employee shares', in relation to a company, means shares of the company which would be relevant shares in it but for the fact that they are held by a person who acquired them in pursuance of an employees' share scheme.

5 'Relevant shares', in relation to a company, means shares in the company other than:

(a) shares which as respects dividends and capital carry a right to participate only up to a specified amount in a distribution, and

(b) shares which are held by a person who acquired them in pursuance of an employees' share scheme or, in the case of shares which have not been allotted, are to be allotted in pursuance of such a scheme.

6 A reference to a class of shares is to shares to which the same rights are attached as to voting and as to participation, both as respects dividends and as respects capital, in a distribution.

7 In relation to an offer to allot securities required by section 89(1) or by any provision to which section 89(3) applies, a reference in sections 89 to 94 (however expressed) to the holder of shares of any description is to whoever was at the close of business on a date, to be specified in the offer and to fall in the period of 28 days immediately before the date of the offer, the holder of shares of that description.

Section 95 – disapplication of pre-emption rights

1 Where the directors of a company are generally authorised for purposes of section 80, they may be given power by the articles, or by a special resolution of the company, to allot equity securities pursuant to that authority as if:

(a) section 89(1) did not apply to the allotment, or
(b) that subsection applied to the allotment with such modifications as the directors may determine;

and where the directors make an allotment under this subsection, sections 89 to 94 have effect accordingly.

2 Where the directors of a company are authorised for purposes of section 80 (whether generally or otherwise), the company may by special resolution resolve either:

(a) that section 89(1) shall not apply to a specified allotment of equity securities to be made pursuant to that authority, or
(b) that that subsection shall apply to the allotment with such modifications as may be specified in the resolution;

and where such a resolution is passed, sections 89 to 94 have effect accordingly.

3 The power conferred by subsection (1) or a special resolution under subsection (2) ceases to have effect when the authority to which it relates is revoked or would (if not renewed) expire; but if the authority is renewed, the power or (as the case may be) the resolution may also be renewed, for a period not longer than that for which the authority is renewed, by a special resolution of the company.

4 Notwithstanding that any such power or resolution has expired, the directors may allot equity securities in pursuance of an offer or agreement previously made by the company, if the power or resolution enabled the company to make an offer or agreement which would or might require equity securities to be allotted after it expired.

5 A special resolution under subsection (2), or a special resolution to renew such a resolution, shall not be proposed unless it is recommended by the directors and there has been circulated, with the notice of the meeting at which the resolution is proposed, to the members entitled to have that notice a written statement by the directors setting out:

(a) their reasons for making the recommendation,
(b) the amount to be paid to the company in respect of the equity securities to be allotted, and
(c) the directors' justification of that amount.

6 A person who knowingly or recklessly authorises or permits the inclusion in a statement circulated under subsection (5) of any matter which is misleading, false or deceptive in a material particular is liable to imprisonment or a fine, or both.

Disclosure Requirements

COMPANIES ACT 1985, SCHEDULE 4

Paragraph 38

1 The following information shall be given with respect to the company's share capital:

(a) the authorised share capital; and
(b) where shares of more than one class have been allotted, the number and aggregate nominal value of shares of each class allotted.

2 In the case of any part of the allotted share capital that consists of redeemable shares, the following information shall be given:

(a) the earliest and latest dates on which the company has power to redeem those shares;
(b) whether those shares must be redeemed in any event or are liable to be redeemed at the option of the company or of the shareholder; and
(c) whether any (and, if so, what) premium is payable on redemption.

Paragraph 39

If the company has allotted any shares during the financial year, the following information shall be given:

. . .

(b) the classes of shares allotted; and
(c) as respects each class of shares, the number allotted, their aggregate nominal value, and the consideration received by the company for the allotment.

Paragraph 40

1 With respect to any contingent right to the allotment of shares in the company the following particulars shall be given:

(a) the number, description and amount of the shares in relation to which the right is exercisable;
(b) the period during which it is exercisable; and
(c) the price to be paid for the shares allotted.

2 In sub-paragraph (1) above 'contingent right to the allotment of shares' means any option to subscribe for shares and any other right to require the allotment of shares to any person whether arising on the conversion into shares of securities of any other description or otherwise.

Members' Resolutions

COMPANIES ACT 1985

Section 378 – extraordinary and special resolutions

1 A resolution is an extraordinary resolution when it has been passed by a majority of not less than three-fourths of such members as (being entitled to do so) vote in person or, where proxies are allowed, by proxy, at a general meeting of which notice specifying the intention to propose the resolution as an extraordinary resolution has been duly given.

2 A resolution is a special resolution when it has been passed by such a majority as is required for the passing of an extraordinary resolution and at a general meeting of which not less than 21 days' notice, specifying the intention to propose the resolution as a special resolution, has been duly given.

3 If it is so agreed by a majority in number of the members having the right to attend and vote at such a meeting, being a majority:

(a) together holding not less than 95% in nominal value of the shares giving that right; or
(b) in the case of a company not having a share capital, together representing not less than 95% of the total voting rights at that meeting of all the members,

a resolution may be proposed and passed as a special resolution at a meeting of which less than 21 days' notice has been given.

A private company may elect (by elective resolution in accordance with section 379A) that the above provisions shall have effect in relation to the company as if for the references to 95% there were substituted references to such lesser percentage, but not less than 90% as may be specified in the resolution or subsequently determined by the company in general meeting.

4 At any meeting at which an extraordinary resolution or a special resolution is submitted to be passed, a declaration by the chairman that the resolution is carried is, unless a poll is demanded, conclusive evidence of the fact without proof of the number or proportion of the votes recorded in favour of or against the resolution.

5 In computing the majority on a poll demanded on the question that an extraordinary resolution or a special resolution be passed, reference is to be had to the number of votes cast for and against the resolution.

6 For purposes of this section, notice of a meeting is deemed duly given, and the meeting duly held, when the notice is given and the meeting held in the manner provided by this Act or the company's articles.

Section 379A – elective resolution of private company

1 An election by a private company for the purposes of:

(a) section 80A (election as to duration of authority to allot shares),
. . .
(d) section 369(4) or 378(3) (election as to majority required to authorise short notice of meeting), or
. . .

shall be made by resolution of the company in general meeting in accordance with this section.

Such a resolution is referred to in this Act as an 'elective resolution'.

2 An elective resolution is not effective unless:

(a) at least 21 days' notice in writing is given of the meeting, stating that an elective resolution is to be proposed and stating the terms of the resolution, and
(b) the resolution is agreed to at the meeting, in person or by proxy, by all the members entitled to attend and vote at the meeting.

2A An elective resolution is effective notwithstanding the fact that less than 21 days' notice in writing of the meeting is given if all the members entitled to attend and vote at the meeting so agree.

3 The company may revoke an elective resolution by passing an ordinary resolution to that effect.

4 An elective resolution shall cease to have effect if the company is re-registered as a public company.

5 An elective resolution may be passed or revoked in accordance with this section, and the provisions referred to in subsection (1) have effect, notwithstanding any contrary provision in the company's articles of association.

Section 380 – registration, etc of resolutions and agreements

1 A copy of every resolution or agreement to which this section applies shall, within 15 days after it is passed or made, be forwarded to the registrar of companies and recorded by him; and it must be either a printed copy or else a copy in some other form approved by the registrar.

2 Where articles have been registered, a copy of every such resolution or agreement for the time being in force shall be embodied in or annexed to every copy of the articles issued after the passing of the resolution or the making of the agreement.

3 Where articles have not been registered, a printed copy of every such resolution or agreement shall be forwarded to any member at his request on payment of five pence or such less sum as the company may direct.

4 This section applies to:

(a) special resolutions;
(b) extraordinary resolutions;
(bb) an elective resolution or a resolution revoking such a resolution;
. . .
(f) a resolution of a company to give, vary, revoke or renew an authority to the directors for the purposes of section 80 (allotment of relevant securities);

5 If a company fails to comply with subsection (1), the company and every officer of it who is in default is liable to a fine and, for continued contravention, to a daily default fine.

6 If a company fails to comply with subsection (2) or (3), the company and every officer of it who is in default is liable to a fine.

7 For purposes of subsections (5) and (6), a liquidator of a company is deemed an officer of it.

Section 381A – written resolutions of private companies

1 Anything which in the case of a private company may be done:

(a) by resolution of the company in general meeting, or
(b) by resolution of a meeting of any class of members of the company,

may be done, without a meeting and without any previous notice being required, by resolution in writing signed by or on behalf of all the members of the company who at the date of the resolution would be entitled to attend and vote at such meeting.

2 The signatures need not be on a single document provided each is on a document which accurately states the terms of the resolution.

3 The date of the resolution means when the resolution is signed by or on behalf of the last member to sign.

4 A resolution agreed to in accordance with this section has effect as if passed:

(a) by the company in general meeting, or
(b) by a meeting of the relevant class of members of the company,

as the case may be; and any reference in any enactment to a meeting at which a resolution is passed or to members voting in favour of a resolution shall be construed accordingly.

5 Any reference in any enactment to the date of passing of a resolution is, in relation to a resolution agreed to in accordance with this section, a reference to the date of the resolution.

6 A resolution may be agreed to in accordance with this section which would otherwise be required to be passed as a special, extraordinary or elective resolution; and any reference in any enactment to a special, extraordinary or elective resolution includes such a resolution.

7 This section has effect subject to the exceptions specified in Part I of Schedule 15A; and in relation to certain descriptions of resolution under this section the procedural requirements of this Act have effect with the adaptations specified in Part II of that Schedule.

Section 381B – duty to notify auditors of proposed written resolution

1 If a director or secretary of a company:

(a) knows that it is proposed to seek agreement to a resolution in accordance with section 381A, and
(b) knows the terms of the resolution,

he shall, if the company has auditors, secure that a copy of the resolution is sent to them, or that they are otherwise notified of its contents, at or before the time the resolution is supplied to a member for signature.

2 A person who fails to comply with subsection (1) is liable to a fine.

3 In any proceedings for an offence under this section it is a defence for the accused to prove:

(a) that the circumstances were such that it was not practicable for him to comply with subsection (1), or
(b) that he believed on reasonable grounds that a copy of the resolution had been sent to the company's auditors or that they had otherwise been informed of its contents.

4 Nothing in this section affects the validity of any resolution.

Section 381C – written resolutions: supplementary provisions

1 Sections 381A and 381B have effect notwithstanding any provision of the company's memorandum or articles, but do not prejudice any power conferred by any such provision.

2 Nothing in those sections affects any enactment or rule of law as to:

(a) things done otherwise than by passing a resolution, or
(b) cases in which a resolution is treated as having been passed or a

person is precluded from alleging that a resolution has not been duly passed.

Schedule 15A – written resolutions of private companies: Adaptation of procedural requirements

Paragraph 2 – introduction

1 In this Part of this Schedule (which adapts certain requirements of this Act in relation to proceedings under section 381A):

(a) a 'written resolution' means a resolution agreed to, or proposed to be agreed to, in accordance with that section, and
(b) a 'relevant member' means a member by whom, or on whose behalf, the resolution is required to be signed in accordance with that section.

2 A written resolution is not effective if any of the requirements of this Part of this Schedule is not complied with.

Paragraph 3 – section 95 (disapplication of pre-emption rights)

1 The following adaptations have effect in relation to a written resolution under section 95(2) (disapplication of pre-emption rights), or renewing a resolution under that provision.

2 So much of section 95(5) as requires the circulation of a written statement by the directors with a notice of meeting does not apply, but such a statement must be supplied to each relevant member at or before the time at which the resolution is supplied to him for signature.

3 Section 95(6) (offences) applies in relation to the inclusion in any such statement of matter which is misleading, false or deceptive in a material particular.

Paragraph 5 – sections 164, 165 and 167 (authority for off-market purchase or contingent purchase contract of company's own shares)

1 The following adaptations have effect in relation to a written resolution:

(a) conferring authority to make an off-market purchase of the company's own shares under section 164(2),
(b) conferring authority to vary a contract for an off-market purchase of the company's own shares under section 164(7), or
(c) varying, revoking or renewing any such authority under section164(3).

2 Section 164(5) (resolution ineffective if passed by exercise of voting rights by member holding shares to which the resolution relates) does not apply; but for the purposes of section 381A(1) a member holding shares to which the resolution relates shall not be regarded as a member who would be entitled to attend and vote.

3 Section 164(6) (documents to be available at company's registered office

and at meeting) does not apply, but the documents referred to in that provision and, where that provision applies by virtue of section 164(7), the further documents referred to in that provision must be supplied to each relevant member at or before the time at which the resolution is supplied to him for signature.

4 The above adaptations also have effect in relation to a written resolution in relation to which the provisions of section 164(3) to (7) apply by virtue of:

(a) section 165(2) (authority for contingent purchase contract), or
(b) section 167(2) (approval of release of rights under contract approved under section 164 or 165).

Paragraph 6 – section 173 (approval for payment out of capital)

1 The following adaptations have effect in relation to a written resolution giving approval under section 173(2) (redemption or purchase of company's own shares out of capital).

2 Section 174(2) (resolution ineffective if passed by exercise of voting rights by member holding shares to which the resolution relates) does not apply; but for the purposes of section 381A(1) a member holding shares to which the resolution relates shall not be regarded as a member who would be entitled to attend and vote.

3 Section 174(4) (documents to be available at meeting) does not apply, but the documents referred to in that provision must be supplied to each relevant member at or before the time at which the resolution is supplied to him for signature.

TAXATION

Distributions

INCOME AND CORPORATION TAXES ACT 1988

Section 210 – bonus issue following repayment of share capital

1 Where a company:

(a) repays any share capital or has done so at any time after 6 April 1965, and
(b) at or after the time of that repayment issues any share capital as paid up otherwise than by the receipt of new consideration,

the amount so paid up shall, except as provided by any provision of the Corporation Tax Acts, be treated as a distribution made in respect of the shares on which it is paid up, except in so far as that amount exceeds the amount or aggregate amount of share capital so repaid less any amounts previously so paid up and treated by virtue of this subsection as distributions.

2 Subsection (1) above shall not apply where the repaid share capital consists of fully paid preference shares:

(a) if those shares existed as issued and fully paid preference shares on 6 April 1965 and throughout the period from that date until the repayment those shares continued to be fully paid preference shares, or
(b) if those shares were issued after 6 April 1965 as fully paid preference shares wholly for new consideration not derived from ordinary shares and throughout the period from their issue until the repayment those shares continued to be fully paid preference shares.

3 Except in relation to a company within paragraph D of section 704, subsection (1) above shall not apply if the issue of share capital mentioned in paragraph (b) of that subsection:

(a) is of share capital other than redeemable share capital; and
(b) takes place after 5 April 1973 and more than ten years after the repayment of share capital mentioned in paragraph (a) of that subsection.

4 In this section:

'ordinary shares' means shares other than preference shares;
'preference shares' means shares:

(a) which do not carry any right to dividends other than dividends at a rate per cent of the nominal value of the shares which is fixed, and
(b) which carry rights in respect of dividends and capital which are comparable with those general for fixed-dividend shares listed in the Official List of the Stock Exchange.

'new consideration not derived from ordinary shares' means new consideration other than consideration:

(a) consisting of the surrender, transfer or cancellation of ordinary shares of the company or any other company or consisting of the variation of rights in ordinary shares of the company or any other company, or
(b) derived from a repayment of share capital paid in respect of ordinary shares of the company or of any other company.

Section 211 – matters to be treated or not to be treated as repayments of share capital

1 Where:

(a) a company issues any share capital as paid up otherwise than by the receipt of new consideration, or has done so after 6 April 1965; and
(b) any amount so paid up does not fall to be treated as a qualifying distribution or, where the issue took place before 6 April 1973, did not fall to be treated as a distribution;

then, except as otherwise provided by any provision of the Corporation Tax Acts, for the purposes of sections 209 and 210, distributions afterwards made by the company in respect of shares representing that share capital shall not be treated as repayments of share capital, except to the extent to which those distributions, together with any relevant distributions previously so made, exceed the amounts so paid up (then or previously) on such shares after 6 April 1965 and not falling to be treated as qualifying distributions or, where the share capital was issued before 6 April 1973, as distributions.

2 Except in relation to a company within paragraph D of section 704, subsection (1) above shall not prevent a distribution being treated as a repayment of share capital if it is made:

(a) more than ten years after the issue of share capital mentioned in paragraph (a) of that subsection; and
(b) in respect of share capital other than redeemable share capital.

3 In subsection (1) above 'relevant distribution' means so much of any distribution made in respect of shares representing the relevant share capital as apart from that subsection would be treated as a repayment of share capital, but by virtue of that subsection cannot be so treated.

4 For the purposes of subsection (1) above all shares of the same class shall be treated as representing the same share capital, and where shares are issued in respect of other shares, or are directly or indirectly converted into or exchanged for other shares, all such shares shall be treated as representing the same share capital.

5 Where share capital is issued at a premium representing new consideration, the amount of the premium is to be treated as forming part of that share capital for the purpose of determining under this Chapter whether any distribution made in respect of shares representing the share capital is to be treated as a repayment of share capital.

6 Subsection (5) above shall not have effect in relation to any part of the premium after that part has been applied in paying up share capital.

7 Subject to subsection (5) above, premiums paid on redemption of share capital are not to be treated as repayments of capital.

Purchase of own shares

Section 219 – purchase by unquoted trading company of own shares

1 References in the Corporation Tax Acts to distributions of a company shall not include references to a payment made by a company on the redemption, repayment or purchase of its own shares if the company is an unquoted trading company or the unquoted holding company of a trading group and either:

(a) the redemption, repayment or purchase is made wholly or mainly for the purpose of benefiting a trade carried on by the company or by any of its 75 per cent subsidiaries, and does not form part of a scheme or arrangement the main purpose or one of the main purposes of which is:

(i) to enable the owner of the shares to participate in the profits of the company without receiving a dividend, or

(ii) the avoidance of tax; and

the conditions specified in sections 220 to 224, so far as applicable, are satisfied in relation to the owner of the shares; or

(b) the whole or substantially the whole of the payment (apart from any sum applied in paying capital gains tax charged on the redemption, repayment or purchase) is applied by the person to whom it is made in discharging a liability of his for inheritance tax charged on a death and is so applied within the period of two years after the death;

and in sections 220 to 224:

'the purchase' means the redemption, repayment or purchase referred to in subsection (1)(a) above; and
'the vendor' means the owner of the shares at the time it is made.

2 Where, apart from this subsection, a payment falls within subsection (1)(b) above, subsection (1) above shall not apply to the extent that the liability in question could without undue hardship have been discharged otherwise than through the redemption, repayment or purchase of shares in the company or another unquoted company which is a trading company or the holding company of a trading group.

Section 220 – conditions as to residence and period of ownership

1 The vendor must be resident and ordinarily resident in the United Kingdom in the year of assessment in which the purchase is made and if the shares are held through a nominee the nominee must also be so resident and ordinarily resident.

2 The residence and ordinary residence of trustees shall be determined for the purposes of this section as they are determined under section 69 of the 1992 Act for the purposes of that Act.

3 The residence and ordinary residence of personal representatives shall be taken for the purposes of this section to be the same as the residence and ordinary residence of the deceased immediately before his death.

4 The references in this section to a person's ordinary residence shall be disregarded in the case of a company.

5 The shares must have been owned by the vendor throughout the period of five years ending with the date of the purchase.

6 If at any time during that period the shares were transferred to the vendor by a person who was then his spouse living with him then, unless that person is alive at the date of the purchase but is no longer the vendor's spouse living with him, any period during which the shares were owned by that person shall be treated for the purposes of subsection (5) above as a period of ownership by the vendor.

7 Where the vendor became entitled to the shares under the will or on the

intestacy of a previous owner or is the personal representative of a previous owner:

(a) any period during which the shares were owned by the previous owner or his personal representatives shall be treated for the purposes of subsection (5) above as a period of ownership by the vendor, and
(b) that subsection shall have effect as if it referred to three years instead of five.

8 In determining whether the condition in subsection (5) above is satisfied in a case where the vendor acquired shares of the same class at different times:

(a) shares acquired earlier shall be taken into account before shares acquired later, and
(b) any previous disposal by him of shares of that class shall be assumed to be a disposal of shares acquired later rather than of shares acquired earlier.

9 If for the purposes of capital gains tax the time when shares were acquired would be determined under any provision of Chapter II of Part IV of the 1992 Act (reorganisation of share capital, conversion of securities, etc.) then, unless the shares were allotted for payment or were comprised in share capital to which section 249 applies, it shall be determined in the same way for the purposes of this section.

Section 221 – reduction of vendor's interest as shareholder

1 If immediately after the purchase the vendor owns shares in the company, then, subject to section 224, the vendor's interest as a shareholder must be substantially reduced.

2 If immediately after the purchase any associate of the vendor owns shares in the company then, subject to section 224, the combined interests as shareholders of the vendor and his associates must be substantially reduced.

3 The question whether the combined interests as shareholders of the vendor and his associates are substantially reduced shall be determined in the same way as is (under the following subsections) the question whether a vendor's interest as a shareholder is substantially reduced, except that the vendor shall be assumed to have the interests of his associates as well as his own.

4 Subject to subsection (5) below, the vendor's interest as a shareholder shall be taken to be substantially reduced if and only if the total nominal value of the shares owned by him immediately after the purchase, expressed as a fraction of the issued share capital of the company at that time, does not exceed 75 per cent. of the corresponding fraction immediately before the purchase.

5 The vendor's interest as a shareholder shall not be taken to be substantially reduced where:

(a) he would, if the company distributed all its profits available for distribution immediately after the purchase, be entitled to a share of those profits, and
(b) that share, expressed as a fraction of the total of those profits, exceeds 75 per cent of the corresponding fraction immediately before the purchase.

6 In determining for the purposes of subsection (5) above the division of profits among the persons entitled to them, a person entitled to periodic distributions calculated by reference to fixed rates or amounts shall be regarded as entitled to a distribution of the amount or maximum amount to which he would be entitled for a year.

7 In subsection (5) above 'profits available for distribution' has the same meaning as it has for the purposes of Part VIII of the Companies Act 1985, except that for the purposes of that subsection the amount of the profits available for distribution (whether immediately before or immediately after the purchase) shall be treated as increased:

(a) in the case of every company, by £100, and
(b) in the case of a company from which any person is entitled to periodic distributions of the kind mentioned in subsection (6) above, by a further amount equal to that required to make the distribution to which he is entitled in accordance with that subsection;

and where the aggregate of the sums payable by the company on the purchase and on any contemporaneous redemption, repayment or purchase of other shares of the company exceeds the amount of the profits available for distribution immediately before the purchase, that amount shall be treated as further increased by an amount equal to the excess.

8 References in this section to entitlement are, except in the case of trustees and personal representatives, references to beneficial entitlement.

Section 222 – conditions applicable where purchasing company is member of group

1 Subject to section 224, where the company making the purchase is immediately before the purchase a member of a group and:

(a) immediately after the purchase the vendor owns shares in one or more other members of the group (whether or not he then owns shares in the company making the purchase), or
(b) immediately after the purchase the vendor owns shares in the company making the purchase and immediately before the purchase he owned shares in one or more other members of the group,

the vendor's interest as a shareholder in the group must be substantially reduced.

2 In subsections (5) to (7) below 'relevant company' means the company making the purchase and any other member of the group in which the vendor owns shares immediately before or immediately after the purchase, but subject to subsection (4) below.

3 Subject to section 224, where the company making the purchase is immediately before the purchase a member of a group and at that time an associate of the vendor owns shares in any member of the group, the combined interests as shareholders in the group of the vendor and his associates must be substantially reduced.

4 The question whether the combined interests as shareholders in the group of the vendor and his associates are substantially reduced shall be determined in the same way as is (under the following subsections) the question whether a vendor's interest as a shareholder in a group is substantially reduced, except that the vendor shall be assumed to have the interests of his associates as well as his own (and references in subsections (5) to (7) below to a relevant company shall be construed accordingly).

5 The vendor's interest as a shareholder in the group shall be ascertained by:

(a) expressing the total nominal value of the shares owned by him in each relevant company as a fraction of the issued share capital of the company,
(b) adding together the fraction so obtained, and
(c) dividing the result by the number of relevant companies (including any in which he owns no shares).

6 Subject to subsection (7) below, the vendor's interest as a shareholder in the group shall be taken to be substantially reduced if and only if it does not exceed 75 per cent of the corresponding interest immediately before the purchase.

7 The vendor's interest as a shareholder in the group shall not be taken to be substantially reduced if:

(a) he would, if every member of the group distributed all its profits available for distribution immediately after the purchase (including any profits received by it on a distribution by another member), be entitled to a share of the profits of one or more of them, and
(b) that share, or the aggregate of those shares, expressed as a fraction of the aggregate of the profits available for distribution of every member of the group which is:
    (i) a relevant company, or
    (ii) a 51 per cent subsidiary of a relevant company,

exceeds 75 per cent of the corresponding fraction immediately before the purchase.

8 Subsections (6) and (7) of section 221 shall apply for the purposes of subsection (7) above as they apply for the purposes of subsection (5) of that section.

9 Subject to the following subsections, in this section 'group' means a company which has one or more 51 per cent subsidiaries, but is not itself a 51 per cent subsidiary of any other company, together with those subsidiaries.

10 Where the whole or a significant part of the business carried on by an unquoted company ('the successor company') was previously carried on by:

(a) the company making the purchase, or
(b) a company which is (apart from this subsection) a member of a group to which the company making the purchase belongs,

the successor company and any company of which it is a 51 per cent subsidiary shall be treated as being a member of the same group as the company making the purchase (whether or not, apart from this subsection, the company making the purchase is a member of a group).

11 Subsection (10) above shall not apply if the successor company first carried on the business there referred to more than three years before the time of the purchase.

12 For the purposes of this section a company which has ceased to be a 51 per cent subsidiary of another company before the time of the purchase shall be treated as continuing to be such a subsidiary if at that time there exist arrangements under which it could again become such a subsidiary.

Section 223 – other conditions

1 Subject to section 224, the vendor must not immediately after the purchase be connected with the company making the purchase or with any company which is a member of the same group as that company.

In this subsection 'group' has the same meaning as it has for the purposes of section 222.

2 Subject to section 224, the purchase must not be part of a scheme or arrangement which is designed or likely to result in the vendor or any associate of his having interests in any company such that, if he had those interests immediately after the purchase, any of the conditions in sections 221 and 222 and subsection (1) above could not be satisfied.

3 A transaction occurring within one year after the purchase shall be deemed for the purposes of subsection (2) above to be part of a scheme or arrangement of which the purchase is also part.

Section 224 – relaxation of conditions in certain cases

Where:

(a) any of the conditions in sections 221 to 223 which are applicable are not satisfied in relation to the vendor, but
(b) he proposed or agreed to the purchase in order that the condition in section 221(2) or 222(3) could be satisfied in respect of the redemption, repayment or purchase of shares owned by a person of whom he is an associate,

then, to the extent that the result is produced by virtue of the purchase, section 219(1)(a) shall have effect as if the conditions in sections 221 to 223 were satisfied in relation to the vendor.

Section 225 – advance clearance of payments by Board

1 A payment made by a company on the redemption, repayment or purchase of its own shares shall be deemed:

(a) to be one to which section 219 applies if, before it is made, the Board have on the application of the company notified the company that they are satisfied that the section will apply; and
(b) to be one to which section 219 does not apply if, before it is made, the Board have on the application of the company notified the company that they are satisfied that the section will not apply.

2 An application under this section shall be in writing and shall contain particulars of the relevant transactions; and the Board may, within 30 days of the receipt of the application or of any further particulars previously required under this subsection, by notice require the applicant to furnish further particulars for the purpose of enabling the Board to make their decision.

3 If a notice under subsection (2) above is not complied with within 30 days or such longer period as the Board may allow, the Board need not proceed further on the application.

4 The Board shall notify their decision to the applicant within 30 days of receiving the application or, if they give a notice under subsection (2) above, within 30 days of the notice being complied with.

5 If particulars furnished under this section do not fully and accurately disclose all facts and circumstances material for the decision of the Board, any resulting notification by the Board shall be void.

Section 226 – returns and information

1 A company which treats a payment made by it as one to which section 219 applies shall within 60 days after making the payment make a return to the inspector giving particulars of the payment and of the circumstances by reason of which that section is regarded as applying to it.

2 Where a company treats a payment made by it as one to which section 219(1)(a) applies, any person connected with the company who knows of any such scheme or arrangement affecting the payment as is mentioned in section 232(2) shall, within 60 days after he first knows of both the payment and the scheme or arrangement, give a notice to the inspector containing particulars of the scheme or arrangement.

3 Where the inspector has reason to believe that a payment treated by the company as one which section 219(1)(a) applies may form part of a scheme or arrangement of the kind referred to therein or in section 223(2), he may by notice require the company or any person who is connected with the company to furnish him within such time, not being less than 60 days, as may be specified in the notice with:

(a) a declaration in writing stating whether or not, according to

information which the company or that person has or can reasonably obtain, any such scheme or arrangement exists or has existed, and
(b) such other information as the inspector may reasonably require for the purposes of the provision in question and the company or that person has or can reasonably obtain.

4 The recipient of a payment treated by the company making it as one to which section 219 applies, and any person on whose behalf such a payment is received, shall if so required by the inspcctor state whether the payment received by him or on his behalf is received on behalf of any person other than himself and, if so, the name and address of that person.

Section 227 – associated persons

1 Any question whether a person is an associate of another in relation to a company shall be determined for the purposes of sections 219 to 226 and 228 in accordance with the following provisions of this section.

2 A husband and wife living together are associates of one another, a person under the age of 18 is an associate of his parents, and his parents are his associates.

3 A person connected with a company is an associate of the company and of any company controlled by it, and the company and any company controlled by it are his associates.

4 Where a person connected with one company has control of another company, the second company is an associate of the first.

5 Where shares in a company are held by trustees (other than bare trustees) then in relation to that company, but subject to subsection (8) below, the trustees are associates of:

(a) any person who directly or indirectly provided property to the trustees or has made a reciprocal arrangement for another to do so,
(b) any person who is, by virtue of subsection (2) above, an associate of a person within paragraph (a) above, and
(c) any person who is or may become beneficially entitled to a significant interest in the shares;

and any such person is an associate of the trustees.

6 Where shares in a company are comprised in the estate of a deceased person, then in relation to that company the deceased's personal representatives are associates of any person who is or may become beneficially entitled to a significant interest in the shares, and any such person is an associate of the personal representatives.

7 Where one person is accustomed to act on the directions of another in relation to the affairs of a company, then in relation to that company the two persons are associates of one another.

8 Subsection (5) above shall not apply to shares held on trusts which:

(a) relate exclusively to an exempt approved scheme as defined in Chapter I of Part XIV, or
(b) are exclusively for the benefit of the employees, or the employees and directors, of the company referred to in that subsection or of companies in a group to which that company belongs, or their dependants (and are not wholly or mainly for the benefit of directors or their relatives);

and for the purposes of this subsection 'group' means a company which has one or more 51 per cent subsidiaries, together with those subsidiaries.

9 For the purposes of subsections (5) and (6) above a person's interest is significant if its value exceeds 5 per cent of the value of all the property held on the trusts or, as the case may be, comprised in the estate concerned, excluding any property in which he is not and cannot become beneficially entitled to an interest.

Section 228 – connected persons

1 Any question whether a person is connected with a company shall be determined for the purposes of sections 219 to 227 in accordance with the following provisions of this section.

2 A person is connected with a company if he directly or indirectly possesses or is entitled to acquire more than 30 per cent of:

(a) the issued ordinary share capital of the company, or
(b) the loan capital and issued share capital of the company, or
(c) the voting power in the company.

3 Where a person:

(a) acquired or became entitled to acquire loan capital of a company in the ordinary course of a business carried on by him, being a business which includes the lending of money, and
(b) takes no part in the management or conduct of the company,

his interest in that loan capital shall be disregarded for the purposes of subsection (2) above.

4 A person is connected with a company if he directly or indirectly possesses or is entitled to acquire such rights as would, in the event of the winding up of the company or in any other circumstances, entitle him to receive more than 30 per cent of the assets of the company which would then be available for distribution to equity holders of the company; and for the purposes of this subsection:

(a) the persons who are equity holders of the company, and
(b) the percentage of the assets of the company to which a person would be entitled,

shall be determined in accordance with paragraphs 1 and 3 of Schedule 18, taking references in paragraph 3 to the first company as references to an equity holder and references to a winding up as including references to any other circumstances in which assets of the company are available for distribution to its equity holders.

5 A person is connected with a company if he has control of it.

6 References in this section to the loan capital of a company are references to any debt incurred by the company:

(a) for any money borrowed or capital assets acquired by the company, or
(b) for any right to receive income created in favour of the company, or
(c) for consideration the value of which to the company was (at the time when the debt was incurred) substantially less than the amount of the debt (including any premium thereon).

7 For the purposes of this section a person shall be treated as entitled to acquire anything which he is entitled to acquire at a future date or will at a future date be entitled to acquire.

8 For the purposes of this section a person shall be assumed to have the rights or powers of his associates as well as his own.

Section 229 – other interpretative provisions

1 In sections 219 to 228:

'control' has the meaning given by section 840;
'holding company' means a company whose business (disregarding any trade carried on by it) consists wholly or mainly of the holding of shares or securities of one or more companies which are its 75% subsidiaries;
'personal representatives' means persons responsible for administering the estate of a deceased person;
'quoted company' means a company whose shares (or any class of whose shares) are listed in the official list of a stock exchange;
'shares' includes stock;
'trade' does not include dealing in shares, securities, land or futures and 'trading activities' shall be construed accordingly;
'trading company' means a company whose business consists wholly or mainly of the carrying on of a trade or trades;
'trading group' means a group the business of whose members, taken together, consists wholly or mainly of the carrying on of a trade or trades, and for this purpose 'group' means a company which has one or more 75 per cent. subsidiaries together with those subsidiaries; and
'unquoted company' means a company which is neither a quoted company nor a 51 per cent subsidiary of a quoted company.

2 References in sections 219 to 228 to the owner of shares are references to the beneficial owner except where the shares are held on trusts (other than bare trusts) or are comprised in the estate of a deceased person, and in such a case are references to the trustees or, as the case may be, to the deceased's personal representatives.

3 References in sections 219 to 228 to a payment made by a company include references to anything else that is, or would but for section 219 be, a distribution.

Purchases and redemptions treated as foreign income dividends

FINANCE ACT 1997, SCHEDULE 7

Paragraph 1 – distributions to which Schedule applies

1 Subject to paragraphs 4 to 7 below, this Schedule applies to any qualifying distribution which:

(a) falls within either or both of sub-paragraphs (2) and (3) below; and
(b) is a distribution made on or after 8th October 1996 by a company resident in the United Kingdom.

2 A qualifying distribution of a company falls within this sub-paragraph if it is a payment made by that company:

(a) on the redemption, repayment or purchase of its own shares, or
(b) on the purchase of rights to acquire its own shares.

. . .

5 In this Schedule:

. . .

'qualifying distribution' has the same meaning as in the Taxes Act 1988;
'shares' has the same meaning as in sections 219 to 228 of that Act (purchase of own shares);

. . .

Paragraph 2 – distributions treated as foreign income dividends

1 The Tax Acts shall have effect, and be deemed in relation to any time on or after 8th October 1996 to have had effect, as if a qualifying distribution to which this Schedule applies were a foreign income dividend within the meaning of Chapter VA of Part VI of the Taxes Act 1988 and, accordingly, as if the making of the distribution were the payment of a foreign income dividend.

. . .

3 Sub-paragraph (1) above has effect subject to:

(a) section 95(1A)(b) of the Taxes Act 1988 (receipt of qualifying distribution by dealer not to be treated as FID for certain purposes); and
(b) section 247(5B) to (5D) of that Act (distributions that are subject to group income elections).

4 Sub-paragraph (2) above has effect in relation to the making of elections on or after 8th October 1996.

Paragraph 3 – distributions treated as section 686 income of trustees

1 This paragraph applies where:

(a) a qualifying distribution to which this Schedule applies by virtue of its falling within paragraph 1 (2) above is or has been made to trustees; and
(b) those trustees are not or, as the case may be, were not the trustees of a unit trust scheme within the meaning of section 469 of the Taxes Act 1988.

2 The relevant part of that distribution (and, accordingly, the corresponding part of the foreign income dividend that paragraph 2(1) above deems the distribution to be) shall be treated for the purposes of the Tax Acts as if it were income to which section 686 of the Taxes Act 1988 (application of rate applicable to trusts to income of certain discretionary trusts) applies.

3 In sub-paragraph (2) above the reference to the relevant part of the distribution is a reference to so much (if any) of that distribution as:

(a) is not income falling within paragraph (a) of section 686(2) of the Taxes Act 1988 (income which is to be accumulated or which is payable at any person's discretion);
(b) does not fall to be treated for the purposes of the Income Tax Acts as income of a settlor;
(c) is not income arising under a trust established for charitable purposes; and
(d) is not income from investments, deposits or other property held for any such purposes as are mentioned in sub-paragraph (i) or (ii) of section 686(2)(c) of the Taxes Act 1988 (property held for pension purposes).

4 Subsection (6) of section 686 of the Taxes Act 1988 (meaning of 'trustees' etc) shall apply for the purposes of this paragraph as it applies for the purposes of that section.

5 This paragraph has effect for the year 1997–98 and subsequent years of assessment and shall be deemed to have had effect for the year 1996–97 in relation to distributions made on or after 5th December 1996.

Stamp Duty

FINANCE ACT 1986

Section 66 – company's purchase of own shares

1 This section applies where a company purchases its own shares under section 162 of the Companies Act 1985 or Article 47 of the Companies (Northern Ireland) Order 1982.

2 The return which relates to the shares purchased and is delivered to the registrar of companies under section 169 of that Act or, as the case may be, Article 53 of that Order shall be charged with stamp duty, and treated for all purposes of the Stamp Act 1891, as if it were an instrument transferring the shares on sale to the company in pursuance of the contract (or contracts) of purchase concerned . . .

Index